CW00809921

30 Days with Davia

Other books in the series:

30 Days with Mary:
A devotional journey with the mother of God

30 Days with Elijah:
A devotional journey with the prophet

30 Days with John:
A devotional journey with the disciple

30 Days with Esther:
A devotional journey with the queen

You can read more about Emily and her books
at:
www.emily-owen.com
facebook.com/EmilyOwenAuthor/
or
twitter.com/EmilyOwenAuthor

30 Days with David

**A devotional journey
with the shepherd boy**

Emily Owen

Authentic

Copyright © 2017 Emily Owen

23 22 21 20 19 18 17   7 6 5 4 3 2 1

First published 2017 by Authentic Media Limited,
PO Box 6326, Bletchley, Milton Keynes, MK1 9GG.
authenticmedia.co.uk

The right of Emily Owen to be identified as the Author of this Work
has been asserted by her in accordance with the
Copyright, Designs and Patents Act 1988.

All rights reserved.
No part of this publication may be reproduced, stored
in a retrieval system, or transmitted in any form or by any means,
electronic, mechanical, photocopying, recording or otherwise, without
the prior permission of the publisher or a licence permitting restricted
copying. In the UK such licences are issued by the Copyright Licensing
Agency, Barnard's Inn, 86 Fetter Lane, London EC4A 1EN.

British Library Cataloguing in Publication Data
A catalogue record for this book is available from the British Library.
ISBN: 978-1-78078-449-6
978-1-78078-451-9 (e-book)

Unless otherwise noted, all Scripture quotations taken from the Holy Bible,
New International Version Anglicised
Copyright © 1979, 1984, 2011 Biblica.
Used by permission of Hodder & Stoughton Ltd, an Hachette UK company.
All rights reserved. 'NIV' is a registered trademark of Biblica UK trademark
number 1448790.

Scripture quotations noted NLT are taken from the Holy Bible,
New Living Translation, copyright © 1996, 2004, 2007, 2013, 2015
by Tyndale House Foundation.
Used by permission of Tyndale House Publishers, Inc.,
Carol Stream, Illinois 60188. All rights reserved.

Scripture quotations noted KJV are taken from The Authorized (King James)
Version. Rights in the Authorized Version in the United Kingdom
are vested in the Crown. Reproduced by permission of the Crown's patentee,
Cambridge University Press.

Cover design by Elena Karoumpali, L1 Graphics
Printed and bound by CPI Group (UK) Ltd, Croydon, CR0 4YY

for my grandad (1926–2015)

John 10:3

Acknowledgements

Thank you to Simon and the team:
your support is invaluable.

Thank you to my family and friends:
you make life better.

Thank you to the children:
repeatedly being asked to sing the David song
(with actions) motivated me so much!

And thank you to God:
always.

Psalm 121

I lift up my eyes to the mountains –
where does my help come from?
My help comes from the LORD,
the Maker of heaven and earth.

He will not let your foot slip –
he who watches over you will not slumber;
indeed, he who watches over Israel
will neither slumber nor sleep.

The LORD watches over you –
the LORD is your shade at your right hand;
the sun will not harm you by day,
nor the moon by night.

The LORD will keep you from all harm –
he will watch over your life;
the LORD will watch over your coming and going
both now and for evermore.

Introduction

'I have found David son of Jesse, a man after my own heart' (Acts 13:22).

God says this.

What does the character of a 'man after God's own heart' look like?

Through David's diary, we begin to see.

David is not perfect.

His life is not perfect.

He has ups and downs, just like anyone else.

Yet, through it all, he keeps his eyes on God.

He knows God is with him.

And he's a man after God's own heart.

Each day's reading ends with 'David's Aim'. This is something for you to keep in mind throughout the day. The 'My response' page is for you to use in any way you choose. Perhaps to record something that drew you closer to God's heart. To God's perspective.

I pray that, as you read and reflect, you will be like David.

Keeping your eyes on God.

Knowing God is with you.

And chasing God's heart.

Emily

Day 1

There's something important going on at home. I'm not there but my brothers are, and my dad. They've all got together because the prophet Samuel has arrived in town. The town elders were really worried when Samuel turned up. They thought it must mean there was trouble or something, but Samuel assured them that he came in peace. Then he consecrated my dad and brothers and invited them to a feast.

Samuel arrives in Bethlehem.
But the place does not exactly welcome him with open arms.
Certainly not at first, anyway.
When the leaders of the town saw Samuel, they were afraid.
They were scared.
He must have come to bring trouble.
Mustn't he?
Eventually, they managed to ask him:
'Samuel, do you come in peace?' (1 Samuel 16:4).

How do people feel when they see you coming?
Do they wonder whether or not you come in peace?
Do they feel a bit wary?
Or is your life such that people feel safe with you?
They don't need to worry or be scared.
Because they know you want the best for them.

Romans 12:18 (NLT):
'Do all that you can to live in peace with everyone.'

And what about God?
How do you feel when you see he comes to you?
Are you glad he's there?
Or do you feel scared?

Let's look at Genesis 3:

Adam and Eve are living in the Garden of Eden.
Paradise.
But, recently, paradise has not been so good.
The fact that they were naked had never occurred to
them.
Until a serpent came along.
A serpent which told them to eat what God had
forbidden.
So they ate.
And immediately realized they were naked.
Which they didn't like.
At all.

So they sewed leaves into clothes for themselves.
But then, they saw something they found much
worse than their own nakedness.
Well, they heard it.
God's footsteps.
Walking in the garden.
He was close by, and Adam and Eve didn't like that.
It made them scared.
So they hid.
And God, knowing full well where they were – just
as he always knows full well where you are – asked
them,
'Where are you?'

Where are you?
You can stop hiding if you want.
I'd like you to.
I'm not going to force you to.
But you never need to hide from me.

Maybe, like Adam and Eve, the thought of God
knowing certain things about you makes you
embarrassed.
Afraid.
Want to hide.

Even though hiding is hard.

God says,
'Where are you?'
You can stop hiding if you want.
Where are you?
Tell me.
Even if you're not afraid or embarrassed.
Tell me anyway.
Because I'm interested.

And you know why?
Do you know why God wants to know where you are?
Do you know why he's interested?
It's to do with how *he* feels when he sees *you* coming.

A man has gone away from his dad (Luke 15).
He's turned his back on him.
And done things he's ashamed of.
But now he wants to be back home.
He's scared, though.
What if his dad doesn't want him back?
Nevertheless, the man trudges on . . .
'And while he was still a long way off, his father
saw him coming. Filled with love and compassion,
he ran to his son, embraced him, and kissed him'
(verse 20 NLT).

You are the son.
And God is the father looking for you.
You.

Day 1

As you begin this journey with David, know that God is looking for you.
Wherever you are.
He's interested.
As he looks,
he sees you.
When he sees you,
he is filled with love and compassion.

God comes in peace.
You can stop hiding.

> *Father God,*
>
> *Thank you that you are looking for me.*
> *You care about where I am.*
> *Help me to accept your love.*
> *Accept your compassion.*
> *And to stop hiding from you.*
> *Because I don't need to hide.*
> *You come in peace.*
>
> *Amen*

David's Aim

Stop hiding

My response:

Day 2

Apart from the fact that I've not been included in the feast, I haven't said much about myself.

My name is David.

My dad's name is Jesse.

I have seven older brothers.

I'm a shepherd from Bethlehem.

I'm not at home much; most of the time I'm with my sheep. Protecting them from attack, or leading them to fresh grass. My life is quite good really, I like it.

Let's look some more at that story in Luke 15:

After the father welcomes his son home with open arms, he decides to throw a party.
A big party.
He gets the best food,
the best clothes,
a brilliant guest list.
The party is in full swing.
Everyone is celebrating.
And then the father notices something.
Someone is missing.

Someone important.
His newly returned son's older brother.

Discovering that his elder son is just outside, the father goes to him.
And he realizes why his son is not coming in.
He can see it written all over his face.
Anger.
Pure anger.
'Please,' says the father.
'Please come and join the party.'
'Why should I?'
'Because your brother has come home!'
'So? Why would I care about that?
'He goes off, wastes all your money, and then you throw him a party just because he's come home now the money has run out?
'Did you miss the fact that I've been here the whole time and you've never thrown a party for me?'

Do you ever think that?
That people don't notice you?
That they miss you in the crowd?

Do you think God misses you in the crowd?

Well, did you know that God even notices every time you sit down?
Or stand up again? (Psalm 139:2).
He won't miss you in a crowd.

God never misses you.
He knows exactly where you are.
Literally and metaphorically.
Right now.

Psalm 121:8 (NLT):

*'The LORD keeps watch over you as you come
and go, both now and forever.'*

The father hadn't missed the older brother, either.
'No, son. I didn't miss it.
'I didn't miss the fact that you are here.'

Luke 15:31:

*' "My son," the father said, "you are always with me,
and everything I have is yours." '*

You are always with me.
I am always with you.
We're always together.
How could I possibly miss you?
Jesus said, 'I am with you always' (Matthew 28:20).
Always.
With.
You.
Every moment.

Everything I have is yours.
The elder son lived as though he had nothing.

Despite his father's assurance that he had everything.
'God will meet all your needs according to the riches
of his glory in Christ Jesus' (Philippians 4:19).
God has given you so much.
Do you live as though he has?
Or do you live as though he hasn't?
Will your God meet your needs?
Or won't he?

The older brother was not only living as though he
didn't have everything.
He was living as though he'd forgotten who he was.
Forgotten that he was the heir to his father's estate.

Don't make the same mistake yourself.
Don't forget who you are.
Your identity.
'See how very much our Father loves us, for he calls us
his children, and that is what we are!' (1 John 3:1 NLT).
You are a child of God.
Your identity is in him.
How does that affect you?

The older brother was invited to the party.
He was invited.
But he chose not to attend.
And he was miserable.
David was not invited to the feast.
He was not included.
He couldn't attend.

And he was content.
Why?
Because, unlike the older brother, he had security in who he was.

God calls us his children.
And that is what we are.

Father God,

Am I like the older brother?
Losing sight of who I am?
Of who you've made me to be?
I'd like to be more like David.
Secure in the identity you've given me.
Knowing that you never miss me in the crowd.
Even when I do.

Amen

David's Aim

I'm God's child

My response:

Day 3

Well, I may not be at the feast but news of it is filtering through. Apparently, Samuel has come to choose and anoint the next king now that King Saul is on his way out. And he's with my brothers right now. Wow, one of them will become king. The king will be my brother. This is my brother, the king. I would think Samuel will go for Eliab. He's the oldest, after all, and he's tall and strong.

1 Samuel 16:1:
'How long will you mourn for Saul, since I have rejected him as king over Israel? . . . be on your way; I am sending you to Jesse'.

Samuel was mourning.
For Saul, the first king of Israel.
Samuel himself had anointed Saul (1 Samuel 10) but now, due to Saul's behaviour, God had rejected him as king.
That's why Samuel was mourning.
Was grieving.
Was sad.

Things were changing.
And change can be hard.

Let's look at John 16:

Jesus is preparing his disciples for change.
For three years, Jesus and his disciples had lived life
together.
The disciples had given up everything to follow Jesus.
And they had no regrets.
It had been an amazing journey.
Full of adventure.
With Jesus right there.
But now the route was changing.
The map was beginning to point in a different
direction.

Jesus told the group, 'I'm going away.'
You won't see me anymore.
I won't be physically walking down the road with you,
or teaching you
or sharing meals with you.
And that was scary.
But, said Jesus.
But . . .
Unless I go, the helper I'm sending you won't come.
And you will really need him.

John 14:16 (NLT):

Jesus said, 'I will ask the Father, and he will give you another Advocate, who will never leave you.'

Jesus is talking about the Holy Spirit.
The advocate, helper, counsellor.
Who would never leave them.
Who will never leave you.
Help is at hand.
All the time.

You're not on your own.
Don't forget it.

How are you at moving on?
From good things as well as bad?
Spending time physically in Jesus' company was definitely a good thing.
But so was what Jesus had in mind next.
The helper who would never leave them.
Saul had once been a good king.
But now it was time to move on.

Isaiah 43:18,19:

'Forget the former things; do not dwell on the past. See, I am doing a new thing! Now it springs up; do you not perceive it? I am making a way in the wilderness and streams in the wasteland.'

Do not dwell on the past.
God's doing a new thing.
Every day (see Lamentations 3:23).
Will you join him?

Sometimes, like Samuel, we look back in mourning,
or nostalgically,
or wistfully.
But, if our eyes are fixed backwards in mourning,
we can't look forward in anticipation.

The disciples, and Samuel, had to let go of the way
things had been.
Let go, so they had hands free to reach for what
would be.

1 Corinthians 2:9 (NLT):
*'No eye has seen, no ear has heard, and no mind has
imagined what God has prepared for those who love him.'*

*'How long will you mourn for Saul, since I have rejected
him as king over Israel?. . .'*
How long will you mourn for what's behind, if God
has rejected it in favour of something new?
Don't miss out.
'. . . be on your way; I am sending you' (1 Samuel 16:1).
On your way.
Into every day.
Sent.

Day 3

Father God,

Moving on can be hard.
Sometimes I'm better at looking backwards.
Not forwards.
Well, a lot of the time, really.
Thank you that you do new things, all the time.
In my life.
And in me.
Help me to keep looking for them.
Please keep me facing in the right direction.

Amen

David's Aim

I'm sent into today

My response:

Day 4

I was wrong. Well, sort of. Samuel did choose Eliab, but God said no. So, then Samuel chose Abinadab, then Shammah and on and on until God had said 'no' to each one of my brothers. It looks as though I won't be brother to the king after all.

Samuel was obedient.
He faced forward and went where God sent him.
So far so good.
He went to the home of the exact family God had chosen.
So far so good.
And then he chose the king.
So far so . . . no.
He's not the one, said God.
Oh. Well how about this one?
Neither's he.
Nor him.
Samuel went through every brother there.
All seven of them.

And God said *no*.
Each time.

The God who had said, *I have chosen one of Jesse's sons to be king* (1 Samuel 16:1b),
said *no*.
Each time.

Let's look at Simeon, Luke 2:

Simeon was old.
Really old.
But he knew he wouldn't die yet.
Day after day he knew it.
Night after night.
Because, day after day, night after night, the promise he was waiting for had not happened.
He'd been told by God that before he died, he'd see a special baby.
Jesus.
But it hadn't happened.

Days passed into weeks.
Weeks into months.
Maybe months passed into years.
Probably, every baby he saw, Simeon thought, 'Is this the one?'
And, every time, the answer was 'no'.
Not this one.
Until, one day, the answer was 'yes'.

Day 4

Simeon kept looking.
Against the odds, he kept believing in what God had
told him.
Samuel did, too.
He asked Jesse, 'Are these all the sons you have?'
Because God hasn't said 'yes' yet.

Samuel didn't let the noes get in the way of the
bigger picture God had painted.
The picture with one of Jesse's sons as king.

God sees the bigger picture.
And the bigger picture is far too huge for us to get
more than a glimpse.
Which means that God sometimes says 'no'.

How do you respond when God says no?

Both Simeon and Samuel responded by continuing to
look for the yes.
Which is just the way it should be.
A great example to follow.
But don't we sometimes respond to God's 'no' by
saying 'no' right back?
No, I won't do it.
I won't keep looking.
I won't wait for the yes.
No, no, no.

Let's look at a 'no' conversation in the Bible,
Exodus 3,4:

Moses: No, God. Please. Can't you ask someone else?
God: No.
I want you to lead my people, Moses.
You.
No one else.
Moses: No, you can't mean it.
God: I do.
Moses: But I stutter. No. Come on, God; I mean, how
can I speak to a crowd of people? Please ask someone
else.
God: No.
And so it goes on.

In the end, what is it that enables Moses to say 'yes' to
God's plan?
'Yes' to God's bigger picture?

Exodus 4:15:
God said, 'I will help . . . you'.

God says the same thing to you:
I will help you.
Through the noes,
I will help you find my 'yes'.
Yes, you can do this.
I promise.

Day 4

Father God,

How do I respond when you say 'no'?
That's a good question.
I do often think I know best.
Help me to remember that you see the bigger picture.
And that whatever you say 'yes' to, you'll help me do.
And through.
I can do this.
Thank you.

Amen

David's Aim

Find God's 'yes'

My response:

Day 5

I've got to go back home. I was really surprised when a messenger rushed up to me just now and told me to get back, fast. Apparently, Samuel is saying that the feast can't start until I get there. I've no idea why but it seems everyone is waiting for me, so I'd better get going.

David was not even considered for king by his own father.
His brothers were.
But not David.
In answer to Samuel's question, 'Are these all the sons you have?' Jesse replies (1 Samuel 16:11):
Well, there is still the youngest.
But he's out in the fields looking after the sheep.
I do have another son, BUT …
In other words,
you won't want to bother with him.
He won't be what you're looking for.

Do you ever feel like that?
That people think you're not worth bothering with?

Or maybe you think other people not worth bothering with?

Let's look at a man in Luke 18:

This man is sitting by the roadside.
He's blind.
And he's begging.
Begging is all he can do.
As he sits there, he hears a noise.
It sounds as though people are crowding around.
'What's going on?' he asks someone.
'Jesus is coming!'
So the man calls out.
'Jesus. Have mercy on me!'
And people tell him to be quiet.
To stop calling.
To just sit there.
Has he forgotten that he's blind?
He needs to remember his place.
A place the crowd think is not even worth them, let alone Jesus, bothering about.
Just be quiet.

But this time the man realizes something.
He realizes he is worth the bother.
He refuses to believe he's wrong to be calling out to Jesus.

Sitting by the road,
surrounded by people, yet
obliterated by darkness,
the man calls out again.
Louder.

'Jesus.
'Have mercy on me!'

In other words,
I'm here.
Notice me.
Please.
I'm here.

Sometimes, we can feel obliterated.
By circumstances.
By other people.
By feelings.
By life.
Overwhelmingly, everything whirls around us.
And we become hidden in darkness.

In the chaos, call out:
I'm here.

Even when you don't know where 'here' is anymore.

The man couldn't see where he was.
He didn't even know for sure that Jesus was there.
He couldn't see Jesus.
And yet he called out.
I'm here.

Call out to God.
Even if you're not sure he's there.

Isaiah 58:9 (NLT):

'Then when you call, the LORD will answer. "Yes, I am here," he will quickly reply.'

What happened after the man called out?
Jesus stopped.
He stopped.
He took note.
And then he asked people to bring the man to him.

Is Jesus asking you to bring anyone near to him?

When the man came close, Jesus asked,
'What do you want me to do for you?' (verse 41).

How would you answer that question from Jesus?
What do you want me to do for you?
What's your heart-longing?

The man says, 'I want to see.'
That's his heart-longing.
To stop being obliterated by darkness.
And Jesus says, *OK*.

God is a God who notices.

He doesn't want you to be obliterated.
By anything.

Darkness.
Circumstances.
Life.

Because, in the midst of it all, he hears you calling.

I'm here.
He knows you are.

The crowd may not have bothered with the man.
But Jesus did.
Jesse may not have bothered about David.
But Samuel did.
Because God did.
That's why Samuel said no one could sit down to eat
until David arrived.

Without David, the celebration could not get started.
Because someone would be missing.
Someone who mattered.
Someone who,
despite apparently not being bothered about,
actually had a vital part to play.

1 Corinthians 12:27 (NLT):

'All of you together are Christ's body, and each of you is a part of it.'

Father God,

You notice me in the crowd.
You hear me when I call.
Thank you.

Amen

David's Aim

I'm here

My response:

Day 6

I'm not sure what to say now. What a day. It seems I am king! Let me just write that again.

I am king.

King David.

How strange that sounds.

A few hours ago, I was sitting on the hills with my sheep, and now I am king. God chose me and Samuel anointed me. My brothers were all there, and my dad. In some ways, it felt as though I was not there. How was this happening to me? But at the same time, I felt a special power from God.

Let's pick up on a question from yesterday.

Is God asking you to bring anyone near?

For Samuel, the answer to that question was definitely 'yes'.

God chose David to be king.

And God chose Samuel to let David know.

To tell David God's plan.

To bring David near.

Let's look at John 1:

Andrew is with Jesus.
Andrew had been told about Jesus, so he decided to follow him.
As Jesus walked along the road, Andrew fell in behind.
When Jesus saw him following, he asked, 'What do you want?'
What do you want, Andrew?
And Andrew replied with a question of his own:
'Where are you staying, Jesus?'
In other words,
I want to know where you are.
Because where you are is where I want to be.
And Jesus said, 'Come on, I'll show you.'

He could have said, *I'm staying over there.*
Go up the road, turn left at the crossroads and it's the
third house on your right.
But he didn't.
He said, *Come on.*
Let's go together.
And you'll see.

Wherever life takes you, Jesus is always there, saying:
Come on.
Let's go together.
And you'll see.

So Andrew went and saw where Jesus was staying.
He spent time with Jesus.
Time.
Time like nothing he'd ever experienced before.
And he thought, 'I've got to tell my brother about Jesus.'
So off he went and found Simon.
And brought him to Jesus.

When they arrived, Jesus looked at Simon.
He didn't say anything.
He just looked.

Simon was seen by Jesus.
He was noticed by Jesus.
Just as the blind man was.
Just as you are.

And then Jesus spoke.
I know who you are.
You're Simon.
I also know who you will be.
Peter.

Simon means the listener.
Peter means the rock.
When Jesus looked at Simon, he saw Simon.
But he also saw potential there.
The potential to be a solid leader.
A sure foundation.

Potential which Jesus would spend the next three
years nurturing.
Drawing out.
Encouraging.

Jesus does the same with you.
When he looks at you, he sees you.
But he also sees who you can become.
He sees your potential.
Even if you don't think you have any.

2 Corinthians 3:18:
*'And we all, who with unveiled faces contemplate
the Lord's glory, are being transformed into his image
with ever-increasing glory'.*

God chose Peter for the job.
And he chose Andrew to bring Simon near.
Near to the place where Simon Peter could begin to
recognize his gifting.
God chose David to be king.
And he chose Samuel to let David know.
To bring David near to the place where he could
begin to recognize his gifting.
Enabled by the strength of God.

Philippians 4:13:
'I can do all this through him who gives me strength.'

Has God chosen you to bring someone near?
Near to him.
Near to where they can begin to recognize who they
are,
whether for the first or fiftieth time?
To recognize the gift they've been given.
And reach for their God-given potential.

Come on.
Let's go together.
And you'll see.

> *Father God,*
>
> *Thank you that you know every person*
> *individually.*
> *Including me.*
> *You see me as I am and yet, at the same time, you*
> *see what I can become.*
> *Help me to come with you and see.*
> *And please show me people I can bring near to you.*
> *So they can come and see, too.*
> *Today, tomorrow, next week . . .*
> *Thank you for potential.*
>
> *Amen*

David's Aim

Come and see

My response:

Day 7

Here I am, back on the hills.

　After he'd anointed me king, Samuel left.
I wasn't really sure what to do next. None of us
was. We all just sort of stood around, looking at
each other. In the end, I thought I might as well go
back to my sheep. After all, I'm still their shepherd.
I came back to them and carried on protecting them
from wolves and lions and anything else that
attacked them.

David has just had a big shock.
His world, all he thought he knew, has been turned
upside down.
He's just been told that, one day, he'll be king.
And now he's not really sure what to do.

Let's look at Peter, in John 13:

Peter has just had a big shock.
His world, all he thought he knew, has been turned
upside down.

Day 7

Jesus, his teacher, his leader, his boss,
is kneeling in front of him.
Wanting to wash Peter's feet.

And Peter is embarrassed.

My feet are not very nice.
Jesus shouldn't have to deal with them.
That's not the boss's role.

Peter looks around.
Where's the servant who usually does this job?
The lowest of low jobs.

'Stop it, Jesus,' says Peter.
'You don't need to wash my feet.'

Jesus looks at Peter.
Then he picks up the towel again.
'Peter, I want to wash your feet.'
And Peter says 'no way'.
Lord, you can't be serious?

But Jesus is.
He is serious.
And he gently begins to wipe Peter's dirty feet.

Matthew 20:28:

'The Son of Man [Jesus] did not come to be served, but to serve'.

Jesus never lost sight of who he was:
The Son of Man
who came to serve.

After his anointing as king, what did David do?
He went back to his sheep.
Back to what he knew.
He'd just been told something life-changing.
And yet he didn't allow that to make him lose sight of
who he was.
He was still a shepherd whose sheep needed looking
after.
Still essentially the same person.
So he returned to his roots.

It can be easy to lose sight of ourselves when new
things happen.
Be they good.
Be they bad.
Events overtake us and we lose sight of the essentials.
And then we start doing things in our own strength.
Our own knowledge.
Like Peter, we think we know better than Jesus.
No; you're not going to wash my feet.
I know best here, Jesus.
Leave it to me.

In John 15, Jesus reminds us not to lose sight of our roots.
We are branches on the vine that is Jesus.
And Jesus tells us what that means:
'Apart from me you can do nothing' (verse 5).

That's what our roots look like.
Remembering that whatever we do, we do it in his strength.
Not our own.
Which is why Philippians 4:13 does *not* say;
'I can do everything.'
Full stop.
It says,
'I can do everything through Christ, who gives me strength' (NLT).
Jesus said to Peter, 'Unless I wash you, you have no part with me' (John 13:8).
Apart from me you can do nothing.
Go back to your roots.
Peter was enabled to humble himself,
to let Jesus near his dirty feet.

David was anointed king,
but he went back to his sheep.
Apart from me you can do nothing.
Go back to your roots.
David was enabled to humble himself and remember the essentials.
The important things.

Apart from me you can do nothing.
Go back to your roots.
Humble yourself.
And see what doing all things in his strength brings
for you.

Father God,

I don't think I know better than you.
Not really.
But I know it sometimes seems that way.
Help me to remember who I am.
A branch on your vine.
Protected by you.
I do know my roots.
Apart from you, I can do nothing.
A part of you, I can do everything.
And yet I forget.
Help me to stop forgetting.
Your strength is all I need.

Amen

David's Aim

Go back to my roots

My response:

Day 8

When I'm with my sheep, I don't spend my whole time fighting. Some days, it's really peaceful. No attacks. No sheep falling down ditches. No urgent message to go and be made king!! Just blue-sky-sun-shining kind of days. On those days, I often play my harp. I love to make music.

What do you do when life calms down a bit?
Or maybe life never seems to calm down.
You rush from one thing to the next, trying to keep all the plates spinning.
There are so many pressures in life.
Work, family, other commitments . . .

Sometimes, Psalm 46:10 can feel impossible.
'Be still, and know that I am God'.
Time to be still?
That would be a fine thing!

Let's look at Exodus 14:

The Israelites' life is anything but calm.
They've been living in slavery to the Egyptians for years.

Following orders.
Working every hour of every day.
Pressure.
Pressure.
Pressure.
And finally, they've escaped.
They're free.
But the Egyptians don't like it.
So they set out in pursuit.
By now, the Israelites had set up camp by the sea.
They looked up and saw the entire Egyptian army
marching towards them.
Army one side.
Sea the other.
Caught in the middle.
No escape.
Pressure, pressure, pressure.

The people are panicking.
They are terrified.
Moses, their leader, has the job of trying to reassure
them.
But what can he say?
The situation is anything but calm.
The approaching army is anything but reassuring.
Moses chooses his words carefully:
'The Lord will fight for you; you need only to be still'
(verse 14).

In the midst of pressure,
pressure,
pressure,
Moses tells the people
to
be
still.

Be still.
Be calm.
On the inside.
By reminding yourself who is with you.
You have someone fighting your corner.
All the time.
Someone who will never leave you.
Outer pressure, inner calm.

Be still, and know that I am God.
In the midst of the whirlwind of life,
you can be still.
You can be calm.
On the inside.
Grab a moment of stillness,
anytime and anywhere,
by reminding yourself that God is God.
By knowing that God is.

God has many names, and one is Jehovah-jireh.
Abraham first used this name for God
(see Genesis 22:14 KJV).

Abraham knew pressure.
God had just asked him to kill his son, Isaac.
Abraham didn't want to.
But he did want to obey God.
He was caught in the middle.
As Abraham reached the pressure-point of actually
holding a knife over his son,
he looked up.
And he saw a ram.
To kill in place of Isaac.

Jehovah-jireh: The Lord will provide.

In the biggest pressure Abraham had ever endured,
the Lord did provide.
Jehovah-jireh.
But if Abraham hadn't looked up, he'd have missed it.

Whatever you are going through, don't forget to
look up.
God will provide all you need.
Look up.
And allow him to be your Jehovah-jireh.
There's no better provider.

The Lord will fight for you; you need only to be still.
Jehovah-jireh.
Be still, and know that I am God.

Father God,

I do feel pressured.
A lot of the time.
Sometimes by life.
Sometimes by my own expectations.
Help me to look up.
To take a breath.
To be still and know that you are God.
Help me to let you be my Jehovah-jireh.

Amen

David's Aim

Be still

My response:

Day 9

I'm not with my sheep now, not playing my harp in the hills. I'm playing it somewhere different. In the palace, to be exact. Saul is still king. He's been having really dark moods and nightmares recently, and he wanted someone to come and play the harp for him, to try to soothe his mind. I was recommended because the Lord is with me. My music does seem to help Saul. I am so glad that people respond to the Lord through my music.

David is at the palace now.
At the request of the king.
Saul needed someone to help and David's music was recommended to him.
What a privilege for David.
But it was not always easy.
Being asked to help was a privilege which required sacrifice.

What about you?
Are you someone people can turn to when they need help?
Need support?

Hebrews 13:16:
*'And do not forget to do good and to share with others,
for with such sacrifices God is pleased.'*

Let's look at Ruth:

Ruth did not marry someone from her home town.
Nor did she marry a native of her own country.
She married Kilion who, with his parents and brother,
had moved to Moab from Bethlehem in order to
escape famine.
Then her father-in-law died.
As did her brother-in-law.
And her husband.
Only her mother-in-law, Naomi, and her sister-in-law,
Orpah, were left.

And then Naomi decides that she wants to return to
Bethlehem.
Ruth and Orpah say they'll go with her.
But, on the journey, Naomi tries to persuade the girls
to turn back.
It's not fair on them, to be lumbered with an old
woman like Naomi.
Orpah turns back.
Ruth, on the other hand, says, 'Don't urge me to leave
you or to turn back from you. Where you go I will go,
and where you stay I will stay. Your people will be my
people and your God my God' (Ruth 1:16).

You can push me away all you like.
But I'm going nowhere.
Where you go, I'll go.
What you go through, I'll go through.
What matters to you, matters to me.

God says the same to you.
You can push me away all you like.
But I'm going nowhere.

Psalm 139:9,10 (NLT):
'If I ride the wings of the morning, if I dwell by the
farthest oceans, even there your hand will guide me,
and your strength will support me.'

Where you go, I'll go.

Joshua 1:5:
'I will never leave you nor forsake you.'

What you go through, I'll go through.

Isaiah 43:2 (NLT):
'When you go through deep waters, I will be with you.'

What matters to you, matters to me.

So, Ruth stays with Naomi, even though Naomi tries
to push her away.

Day 9

Naomi is hurting and bitter.
Pushing people away has become automatic.
Ruth refuses to be pushed.
She digs her heels in.
And she stays.
Where you stay, I will stay.
Together.

Ruth needed grace to stay when Naomi was
ungracious.
Grace to accept being pushed away.
Grace to love Naomi in her hurting.
Naomi's hurting.
And Ruth's.

Maybe Ruth sometimes felt that she couldn't keep
sharing herself with Naomi.
Felt that she couldn't keep doing good.
She just couldn't do it anymore.
Maybe you feel like that?
God says:
'My grace is sufficient for you' (2 Corinthians 12:9).

Naomi would later realize that she could not have had
better support than the support she had in Ruth.
Ruth is an example of loyalty.
She stuck by Naomi.

Saul realized that he would not find a better harpist
than David.

It was not always easy to play the harp for Saul, as we will see.
But David, too, was an example of loyalty.
He stuck by Saul.

Perhaps it is not surprising, then, that Ruth was David's great-grandmother.

What faith-traits do you pass on to people?
What faith-traits *will* you pass on to people?

2 Timothy 1:5 (NLT):

'I remember your genuine faith, for you share the faith that first filled your grandmother Lois and your mother, Eunice. And I know that same faith continues strong in you.'

Father God,

I need grace.
I know I can be ungracious.
When I push people away.
Or when they push me away.
Help me to give and accept support.
Accept loyalty.
With other people.
And with you.

Amen

David's Aim

Be gracious

My response:

Day 10

I think Saul likes having me around. He's made me one of his armour-bearers. Basically, that means I sometimes go with him and carry the weapons he needs when he goes to war. We are at war and being attacked right now, by a nation called the Philistines.

A man is walking along.
Staggering.
Limping.
Tripping over.
But he keeps going.
Carrying his heavy load.
He's in no fit state to be carrying anything.
He's just been beaten up.
Tortured.
And now his torturers are forcing him to carry this load.
Staggering along the road, he tries.
He trips.
But he tries.
He's surrounded by a crowd.
Every person is looking at him.

But no one offers to help.
And on he staggers.
Falling more frequently now.
Until finally, he doesn't get up.
Because he can't.
He's too exhausted.
The crowd come to an abrupt halt all around him.
But he just lies there.
On the ground.
Energy gone.
Exhausted.
Until he feels the load being lifted.
Someone is carrying it for him.
He gets to his feet.
Somehow, keeping going is more manageable with someone else sharing the load.

The man is Jesus.
Carrying his cross.

Hebrews 4:15 (NLT):
*'This High Priest of ours understands our weaknesses,
for he faced all of the same testings we do, yet
he did not sin.'*

Jesus knows what it's like to be crushed under a burden.
Jesus knows what it's like to have someone help carry that burden.

And Jesus knows what it's like to accept that help.
He didn't refuse to let anyone else carry the cross.
Of course, no one else could ultimately hang on the cross.
And die the death Jesus died.
But that didn't mean there couldn't be some sharing of the load.

If Jesus could share some of his burdens, perhaps you can too?

Galatians 6:2 (NLT):
'Share each other's burdens, and in this way obey the law of Christ.'

The thing is, something often prevents us from sharing burdens.
Perhaps we don't know there's a burden to be shared.
People don't tell us.
We don't tell them.
So we don't share each other's burdens.
And maybe, because we don't share, we are actually choosing not to obey the law of Christ.

Jesus shared his burden with one person out of the whole crowd.
Sharing does not have to mean telling everyone.

Ecclesiastes 4:9,10 (NLT):

'Two people are better off than one . . . If one person falls, the other can reach out and help. But someone who falls alone is in real trouble.'

But, when Jesus was hanging on that cross, no one could share his burden.
No one.
The burden of being crushed by the sin of the whole world was his alone.
No one could share it.
No one.
Not even God the Father.
'My God, my God, why have you forsaken me?' (Matthew 27:46).
And, because no one could share it, because Jesus dealt with it all on the cross, we can live in the reality of Psalm 55:22 (NLT):

'Give your burdens to the LORD, and he will take care of you.'

David was tasked with carrying Saul's weapons.
Saul was, to all intents and purposes, OK.
He was marching off to war.
Doing his job.
Yet David still carried his weapons.
The weapons which would enable Saul to do his job.

Saul could probably have carried the weapons himself.
Yet David received the honour of carrying them for him.
Being armour-bearer to the king was an honour.
And it was probably nice for Saul to get a bit of a break.
It probably meant he was fresher for battle when he arrived.

So Saul gave to David by honouring him.
David gave to Saul by giving him a break.
David received honour.
Saul received a break.
Neither essential, perhaps.
But both valued.

Acts 20:35:

'The Lord Jesus himself said: "It is more blessed to give than to receive."'

In an amazing paradox, it is impossible to truly give without also receiving.
Receiving blessing.
Try it.
Give without expectation.
And you'll see blessings heading your way.

Day 10

Father God,

Thank you that Jesus set an example.
I can't do everything on my own.
I know that.
But I am stubborn.
And independent.
And not very good at accepting help.
Help me to follow Jesus' example and share my burdens.
With other people.
And with you.

Amen

David's Aim

Give without
expectation

My response:

Day 11

Goliath.

That's the only name on people's lips at the moment. Apparently, he's the hero of the Philistine army. He's massive, over nine feet tall, from what I hear. Everyone is terrified of him, including all our army.

The people had one thought which overshadowed everything else.
Goliath.

Let's look at Luke 10:

Martha has invited Jesus into her home.
Jesus is there right now.
In her house.
He's sitting in her room.
Some others are there, too.
Including Mary, Martha's sister.
Mary is sitting with Jesus, listening to all he is saying.
Martha is dashing around, trying to get everything ready for the meal.
Perhaps she's listening to Jesus with half an ear.

Perhaps she's catching snatches of his sentences as she rushes to and fro.
Or perhaps not.
Guest list? Check.
Set the table? Check.
Put the vegetables on to cook? Check.
Make sure everyone has enough to drink? Check.
Keep an eye on the time? Check.
Tidy away any mess? Check.
Welcome everyone with a smile? Check.
Doing, doing, doing.

Doing was dominating Martha's life.
Overshadowing everything else.
Doing.

And then, during one of her trips through the living room to the table, Martha sees Mary.
Sitting there.
Just sitting.
While Martha herself is run ragged.
And something inside Martha snaps.
Instead of going to the table, she marches up to where Jesus is sitting:
'Lord, don't you care that my sister has left me to do the work by myself? Tell her to help me!' (verse 40).

Tell her to help me.
'Doing' dominated Martha's life.

And she demanded Jesus be part of her doing.
By telling him what to do.

Do you tell him what to do?
Tell her to help me.
Or do you invite him to teach you what to do?
Help me.

Psalm 86:11:

*'Teach me your way, L*ORD*, that I may rely on your faithfulness; give me an undivided heart, that I may fear your name.'*

Let's look at how Jesus addresses Martha's concerns: 'Martha, Martha, you are worried and upset about many things, but few things are needed – or indeed only one. Mary has chosen what is better, and it will not be taken away from her.'

'Lord, don't you care?'
'Martha, Martha.'
I care enough to call you by name.
The first four words Martha uttered here were a contradiction.
'Lord, don't you care?'
He cares.
By definition.

Isaiah 43:1 (NLT):
'I have called you by name.'

In her frustration, Martha didn't call Mary by her name.
My sister . . .
Don't let things get in the way of you seeing people as individuals.
Seeing who they are.
Seeing God as he is.
People are more important than things.
And God is even more important.

. . . has left me to do all the work by myself.
Had Mary left her to it?
Or had Martha decided to do it?
Doing came first.
But Jesus reminded her that only one thing was needed.

Just spend time with me, Martha.
Everything else is getting in the way of you and me.
If the table doesn't look perfect, we'll survive.
If we don't spend time together, we won't survive.
Because there'll be no 'we'.

The Israelites were allowing Goliath to eclipse God.
Martha was allowing 'doing' to eclipse Jesus.
What about you?

As you look at your life, is God big?
The biggest?
Is he in the shadow of other things?
Or are other things in his shadow?
'Mary has chosen what is better, and it will not be
taken away from her.'

Psalm 91:1 (NLT):
*'Those who live in the shelter of the Most High will find
rest in the shadow of the Almighty.'*

Father God,

*When other things threaten to overshadow you,
help me to remember that only one thing is
needed.
Letting you cast the shadow over everything else.
Including me.
And then I can truly rest in you.*

Amen

David's Aim

Rest in God's shadow

My response:

Day 12

Goliath is terrifying! Even the soldiers are petrified when they see him, and they've seen him every morning for the past forty days. Apparently he comes and shouts at them to send a man to fight him. Basically, this one-on-one will decide which army wins, so the idea is for Israel to choose one man to represent them. But no one will do it. Goliath is way too scary and fighting him is too much for anyone in our army to take on.

Only one person was needed.
One person to fight Goliath.
But no one would do it.
In amongst a crowd of people, there was no one.
No one who was willing to risk near-certain death by fighting the giant.

Let's look at Samson, Judges 13 – 16:

Samson is strong.
Incredibly strong.
Stronger than anyone.
Because he's never cut his hair.

In obedience to God.

One day, while Samson is asleep, his girlfriend cuts his hair.

Shaves it off.

And, when Samson wakes, he is weak.

'His strength left him' (Judges 16:19).

So his enemies captured him very easily.

They scratched his eyes out, put him in shackles and sent him to prison.

But, in prison, Samson's hair began to grow back.

Samson was in prison.

He was trapped.

Caught in circumstances beyond his control.

And yet, in those circumstances, his hair began to grow.

His strength grew.

The Israelite army was trapped.

They were caught in circumstances beyond their control.

How could they have known they'd be threatened by Goliath?

By a giant?

And yet, they were.

As they lived their circumstances, their terror began to grow.

As you live your circumstances, what grows in you?
Strength?
Or terror?

Samson had no control over making his hair grow.
Only God could do that.
But Samson didn't shave it off.
He allowed God to grow strength in adversity.

Samson was blind.
He couldn't see his prison walls.
So he couldn't focus on them.
The Israelites could see their enemy.
Could see the giant.
And that's what they focused on.
If you want strength to grow in you, not terror, be careful what you focus on.
Look away from the big, scary giants in your life.
Worries, busyness, health, family, finances . . .
And focus on the one who is bigger than them all.

Hebrews 12:1,2:

'Let us throw off everything that hinders . . . let us run with perseverance the race marked out for us, fixing our eyes on Jesus'.

One day Samson's enemies were throwing a party.
They were in high spirits and wanted some entertainment.

So they dragged Samson out.
Samson stood, unseeing, before them.
He reached out his hands until he felt the pillars
which supported the building.
Then he pushed with all his strength.
And the building came crashing down.
Everyone died.
Including Samson.

Jesus said to Martha, 'few things are needed – or
indeed only one'.
In Samson's case, the 'one thing' was a strong man.
Samson destroyed the Philistine enemy.
And he destroyed himself as well.

Another time, God said only one thing is possible.

One way to reconcile humanity and God.
One way to knock down the barrier between them.
Sinlessness to overcome sin.

Jesus.
Perfection in an imperfect world.
Jesus.
Destroyer of death.
Jesus.
Giver of life.
Jesus.

2 Corinthians 5:17 (NLT):
'Anyone who belongs to Christ has become a new person. The old life is gone; a new life has begun!'

Father God,

My giants are big.
Even bigger than Goliath.
But they are not bigger than you.
They're not.
Help me to fix my eyes on you.
To look away from terror.
And focus on strength.

Amen

David's Aim

See God's strength

My response:

Day 13

Three of my brothers, the oldest ones, have joined Saul's army, so they're being faced with this Goliath every day. I'm not Saul's armour-bearer this time, I'm back home. After all, my sheep still need me and I need my time with them. I split my time between serving Saul and being with my sheep.

Jesse's three oldest sons followed Saul but 'David went back and forth from Saul to tend his father's sheep at Bethlehem' (1 Samuel 17:15).

Let's look at 1 Kings 19:

Elijah is sitting under a tree.
In the middle of the desert.
He doesn't live there.
He's just run there.
Or, more accurately, escaped there.
Queen Jezebel doesn't like Elijah very much.
She doesn't like the fact that he goes around trying to show people God's way.
Because she doesn't want to be reminded of God's way.

It doesn't suit her.
Why should she listen to that annoying little man,
Elijah?
The one who challenges her to change the way she
lives her life?
In fact, she reasons, the best way to live *her* life is to
take *Elijah's* life.

1 Thessalonians 5:11 (NLT):
*'Encourage each other and build each other up, just as
you are already doing.'*

By encouraging people, we help them live.
By not encouraging them, we may hinder their living.
Taking some life from them.
Squeezing it out.
That's not the best way for us to live our lives.
'Encourage each other'.
The verse goes on:
'just as you are already doing.'
Are you?

Jezebel certainly wasn't.
Which is why Elijah has been running.
And, all run out, why he's sitting in the desert.
Under a tree.
He has nothing left.
And so, sitting there,
dishevelled from running,

panting hard and out of breath,
he says to God: 'I've had enough'.

I've had enough.

Let's have a look at what God does *not* say in
response.
He does not say:
'Don't be silly.
Snap out of it.
Call yourself a Christian?
There are people worse off than you.
Count your blessings.'

I've had enough.
Have you had enough?
Enough of trying to escape your situation?
Or enough of not trying to escape your situation?
Tell God.
This is hard.
I've had enough.

God sent an angel to give Elijah food:
'Get up and eat, for the journey is too much for you'
(verse 7).

Matthew 11:28:
*'Come to me, all you who are weary and burdened,
and I will give you rest.'*

After rest and food, Elijah travels on until he reaches
the mountain of God.
And there he stops.
He's been persecuted by Jezebel for a long time.
Now he takes time on the mountain of God.
Easier if he'd done that before he burned out.

'David went back and forth from Saul to tend his
father's sheep at Bethlehem.'
Life with Saul in the royal household was probably
quite busy.
Quite full-on.
And David balanced that by spending time with his
father's sheep.

Life can be busy.
It's a good idea to find a balance.
Pressure/Relaxation.
Busyness/Rest.
Serving/Receiving.

For David, getting the balance meant spending time
with his father's sheep.
How important is ensuring you spend time with your
Father's sheep to you? (John 10).
Meeting with other Christians.
Recharging batteries.
Physical and spiritual.
Encouraging and being encouraged.

Hebrews 10:25 (NLT):

'Let us not neglect our meeting together, as some people do, but encourage one another'.

Remember, David had been anointed king.
Pretty amazing.
And yet he kept his feet on the ground.
He didn't lose perspective.
Of himself.
Or of who he was before God.
And spending time with his father's sheep enabled him to go out and live the life God had given him.
Gave him strength.
As did spending time on the mountain of God for Elijah.

Isaiah 40:31:

'Those who hope in the LORD will renew their strength. They will soar on wings like eagles; they will run and not grow weary, they will walk and not be faint.'

Father God,

I've had enough.
I'm burned out.
I want to balance out.
I need time.
With you.
On your mountain.
And I need people to meet with me there.
More than that.
I need people to remind me how to get there
in the first place.
I've had enough.
Please renew my strength.

Amen

David's Aim

Beware of burnout

My response:

Day 14

Dad has asked me to take some food and stuff to my brothers and see how they are. He wants to know they're OK. So I'll soon be on my way to the front line. Not to be Saul's armour-bearer, just to see my brothers. I guess I might get a glimpse of Goliath, as well.

Jesse, left at home, is wondering how his sons are.
He can't go to them himself.
He's needed at home.
He's stuck at home.
But that doesn't mean his heart is.
Jesse's heart is with his sons.
So he asks David to go and find out how they are doing.
And let him know.
Take some things for them, too.
But ask how they are.

How are you?
It's a good question to ask.
Let's look at some verses in Philippians:

'If the Lord Jesus is willing, I hope to send Timothy to you soon for a visit. Then he can cheer me up by telling me how you are getting along. I have no one else like Timothy, who genuinely cares about your welfare. All the others care only for themselves and not for what matters to Jesus Christ. But you know how Timothy has proved himself' (Philippians 2:19–22a NLT).

Where was Paul when he wrote this letter to the church at Philippi?
He was in prison.
In prison.
And yet he was thinking of others.
Jesse was stuck at home.
And yet he was thinking of others.
Outward-looking.

Philippians 2:4 (NLT):
'Don't look out only for your own interests, but take an interest in others, too.'

Paul certainly took an interest in others.
That's why he was in prison.
For sharing the gospel.
For wanting other people to know Jesus.

But, crucially, Paul did not forget to look out for his own interests as well.
The verse does not say don't look out for yourself.
It says don't *only* look out for yourself.

And why, on this occasion, does Paul say he is thinking of others?
To cheer himself up.
He's in a dark place.
And he needs others to cheer him.
To encourage him.
To help him keep going.

1 Thessalonians 5:11:
'Encourage one another and build each other up'.

But Paul would only be encouraged if the Philippians actually told him, via Timothy, how they were.

Sometimes when people ask, 'How are you?' they're not just being polite.
They're asking because they really want to know.
Are you one of those people?

Let's think about Timothy.
According to Paul, Timothy is different.
He's not like the others.
He genuinely cares.
Not shallowly.
Genuinely.
And Paul has noticed that.

Is genuine care something people notice in you?

What does Paul say genuine care looks like?
It looks like caring about what matters to Jesus.
And what does matter to Jesus?

Mark 12:28–31:
*'One of the teachers of the law . . . asked him [Jesus], "Of
all the commandments, which is the most important?"
"The most important one," answered Jesus, "is this:
'Hear, O Israel: the Lord our God, the Lord is one. Love
the Lord your God with all your heart and with all your
soul and with all your mind and with all your strength.'
The second is this: 'Love your neighbour as yourself.'
There is no commandment greater than these."'*

Love God.
Love him with everything that you have.
Love him with everything that you are.

Jesse loved his sons with what he had: he sent them
food.
Jesse loved his sons with who he was: their caring
father.
Who are you?
And do you love God with who you are?
With your heart:
'Grant me purity of heart, so that I may honor you'
(Psalm 86:11 NLT).
With your soul:
'Praise the LORD, my soul; all my inmost being, praise
his holy name' (Psalm 103:1).

With your mind:
'Take captive every thought to make it obedient to
Christ' (2 Corinthians 10:5).
With your strength:
'He [God] said to me, "My grace is sufficient for
you, for my power is made perfect in weakness."
Therefore . . . when I am weak, then I am strong'
(2 Corinthians 12:9,10).

If we truly love God with all that we are, then perhaps
we begin to reach for Micah 6:6–8 (NLT):

Micah 6:6–7 (NLT)
'What can we bring to the LORD?
Should we bring him burnt offerings?
Should we bow before God Most High
with offerings of yearling calves?
Should we offer him thousands of rams
and ten thousand rivers of olive oil?
Should we sacrifice our firstborn children
to pay for our sins?'

Jesse only asked for one thing from his soldier sons.
A report on how they were.
He didn't ask for souvenirs from the battleground.
Things from them.
External things.

No.
Jesse cared about how they were as people.

God is the same.

Micah 6:8 (NLT)
'No, O people, the LORD has told you what is good,
and this is what he requires of you:
to do what is right, to love mercy,
and to walk humbly with your God.'

Father God,

Thank you for the people you have put in my life.
May I truly care for them.
Not what they have, or what they do,
but them as people.
When I ask, 'How are you?'
I want to mean it.
And please help me love you as I should.
Holding nothing back.
Of things.
Or of me.
I love you with all I am.

Amen

David's Aim

Love God with
all of me

My response:

Day 15

I left really early this morning because I wanted to get a good start. I've got a long journey ahead before I reach the battlefield. I've left someone watching my sheep and I've arrived at the army camp. I left the provisions with the man who looks after the supplies and looked for my brothers.
As I was on my way to find them, there was so much going on . . . people everywhere, war cries, commotion, both sides getting ready to face each other . . . I had to force my way through to get to my brothers.

The second thing Jesus commanded yesterday is 'Love your neighbour as yourself.'
In order to love our neighbour as our self, we need first to learn how to love ourselves.

Let's look at Daniel's story in the book of Daniel:

Daniel is doing well.
Very well.
In fact, King Darius has plans for Daniel.

He plans to put Daniel in charge of the whole kingdom.

Daniel is already in the top three, but soon he'll be second only to the king.

Until, that is, the other government officials heard of it.

And didn't like it very much.

They tried to trap Daniel,

to plot against him,

to catch him out.

Anything to make Daniel look bad in front of the king.

But nothing worked.

Nothing.

So they sat down and thought.

How would they catch Daniel out?

And then it came to them.

Daniel followed God.

Daniel would allow nothing to come between him and his God.

So, what if they persuaded the king to order all the people to pray to the king himself?

That would go against everything Daniel believed in.

The punishment for praying to any god or man, other than the king, would be getting thrown into a den of lions.

In other words, death.

And a horrible death at that.

So they set to work.

Day 15

They did persuade the king.
And then they waited.
What would Daniel do?

Well, Daniel just got on with his life.
He carried on as usual.
And 'usual' included prayer.
Three times a day, Daniel would spend time with God.
Talking things over.
Keeping perspective.

Do you make time for God in your day?

1 Chronicles 16:11:
'Look to the LORD and his strength; seek his face always.'

Now, despite having been ordered not to pray to God,
Daniel continued praying.
Three times a day,
he knelt in front of an open window,
and he talked to God.
Two things the Bible says were in Daniel's prayers
(Daniel 6:10,11):
Saying thank you to God.
Asking God for help.

Thank you, God, for . . .
Please help with . . .

Spies watched Daniel.
He was seen as he prayed.
He was caught.
He was taken.
He was thrown to the lions.
And God saved him.
But the point is, Daniel did look out for himself.
He did 'love himself'.
By making sure he looked after what mattered.
He didn't lose perspective.
Didn't become overwhelmed and distracted by what
was happening in his life.
He set aside time to focus on God.
God and Daniel time.

Thank you, God, for . . .
Please help with . . .

The Daniel way of praying is a good one to follow.
And his prayers were answered.
Remember how Daniel daily asked God for help?
Well, God certainly helped him.
He was not hurt by the lions.
He still had to go among them.
But he was not harmed.

Daniel, before he went out into daily life, made sure
that he was safe.
By protecting himself through prayer.

2 Thessalonians 3:3:

'The Lord is faithful, and he will strengthen you and protect you from the evil one.'

Loving ourselves is being centred in God.
And, when God is our centre, we will truly love our neighbour.

David's heart was centred on God.
And David loved his neighbour.
The battlefield didn't cause him to lose perspective.
By not losing his aim of seeing his brothers, David demonstrated his love for them.
He'd come to see his brothers, and that's what he did.
He really did.
Undivided time with them.

How good are you at giving people your undivided attention?

It's easy to get distracted.
From ourselves.
From other people.
From God.

Luke 10:41,42:

'You [Martha] are worried and upset about many things, but few things are needed – or indeed only one. Mary has chosen what is better, and it will not be taken away from her.'

Don't lose perspective in life.
Choose what is better . . .

Father God,

If I want to love other people, I need to love myself.
Please help me to do that.
I do get distracted easily.
I'm always on the go.
Help me to pause.
To pray.
To gain perspective.
And to keep it.
Thank you . . .
Please help . . .

Amen

David's Aim

Choose love

My response:

Day 16

I've just seen Goliath! He wasn't hard to spot. He really is tall. Anyway, I didn't have to look over many heads as the Israelite army are busy trying to run away from him. Goliath was shouting his usual 'Come and fight me' line but no one answered him. I can't believe it! I asked someone what's the reward for killing Goliath. Apparently, whoever does it will marry Saul's daughter, the princess, and be given great wealth, plus his family will never have to pay taxes again. That's how serious the threat of Goliath is.

Goliath is tall.
He's over nine feet tall.
He stands head and shoulders above everyone else.
He was easy to spot, even in a crowd.
Even easier once the terrified Israelite army had run away from Goliath as fast as they could.
Leaving nothing in the way of seeing Goliath.
No crowds for David to see around or over.
Just direct sight of Goliath.

Let's look at a woman who worked her way through crowds, Mark 5:

Day 16

People were crowding around.
Jesus was in the crowd.
Somewhere.
So was a woman who desperately wanted to get to Jesus.
But, other than perhaps a glimpse now and then, she couldn't see him.
The crowd got in the way and she couldn't fight her way through.
People got in the way.
As they whirled around her, pushing and shoving, so her thoughts raced around her mind.
And perhaps she hesitated.

It might be best if I just sneak up to Jesus.
Try and touch the bottom of his coat or something.
Secretly.
After all, why would Jesus be interested in me?
No one else is.
Even the doctors can't help.
My health is getting worse, not better.
I'm just a no-hoper.
Feelings got in the way.

I've spent all my money on doctors.
Trying to get help.
But help never comes.
I've sold all I owned.
Now I have nothing.

Nothing.
And it's hard.
Things – or lack of things – got in the way.

In the end, the woman did get through to Jesus.
She worked through her crowds:
Crowds of people getting there first.
Crowds of feelings trying to put her down.
Crowds of things whose absence reminded her that
no matter how hard she tried, she couldn't fix this by
herself.
Couldn't make her own life better.
She fought her way through all of them.

Do crowds get in the way of you seeing God?
Crowds of people?
Crowds of feelings?
Crowds of things?

People: 'You are precious [to me]' (Isaiah 43:4).
You.
Feelings: 'You are honored, and I love you' (verse 4, NLT).
You're not a no-hoper.
Things: 'God who takes care of me will supply all
your needs from his glorious riches . . . in Christ Jesus'
(Philippians 4:19 NLT).
You don't need to do it all by yourself.

And she got more than a glimpse of Jesus.
She had a conversation with him.
The woman saw Jesus face-to-face.

Jeremiah 29:13 (NLT):
'If you look for me wholeheartedly, you will find me.'

The reward for fighting Goliath would be marriage to
the king's daughter.
Becoming part of the king's family.

The reward for fighting through our crowds,
feelings,
things,
to get to Jesus,
the reward for wanting more than a glimpse of him,
the reward for letting nothing get in the way of him,
again and again,
is living as his child.
And knowing peace.

Jesus said to the woman who'd fought through,
'Daughter . . . Go in peace' (Mark 5:34).

As he says to you,
Son, daughter . . . Go in peace.
Live in peace.
Accept peace.
Know peace.

Numbers 6:24–26:

'The Lord bless you and keep you; the Lord make his face shine on you and be gracious to you; the Lord turn his face towards you and give you peace.'

Father God,

I'm surrounded by crowds.
Crowds that keep me from you.
I do glimpse you every now and then.
So I do know you're there.
But, Lord, I want to more than glimpse you.
I want to see you face-to-face.
Help me fight through my crowds.
And know peace.

Amen

David's Aim

Lose the crowds

My response:

Day 17

I've just been shoved to one side by Eliab. I guess he'll always be the big brother. This time, he's annoyed with me for speaking! He's mad that I'm talking with some of the other soldiers. He wants to know why I'm there, and who is looking after the few – yes, he said 'few' – sheep in the desert. And he's saying I'm big-headed and my heart is wicked.

When Samuel was choosing the next king, he went straight for Eliab.
Tall, strong, handsome Eliab.
But, apart from 'no', what did God say in response to that choice?
'But the LORD said to Samuel, "Don't judge by his appearance or height, for I have rejected him. The LORD doesn't see things the way you see them. People judge by outward appearance, but the LORD looks at the heart"' (1 Samuel 16:7 NLT).
The Lord, the see-er of hearts, looked straight at Eliab's heart.
And straight at David's heart.
And he chose David.

Because David's heart was perfect?
No.
God chose David's heart because it turned towards
God's own heart.

Acts 13:22:

*'I have found David son of Jesse, a man after my own
heart. He will do everything I want him to do.'*

Is your heart turned towards God?
Sharing, loving, wanting what he wants?

Proverbs 4:23:

*'Above all else, guard your heart, for everything you do
flows from it.'*

But what does Eliab have to say about the heart God
chose? (1 Samuel 17:28).
He says it's wicked.
It's bad.
Not good.
God chose David's heart.
But Eliab called it wicked.

How do you treat things God has chosen?
What has God chosen?
He's chosen you.

Jeremiah 1:5 (NLT):
'I knew [chose] you before I formed you in your mother's womb.'

Before you did anything at all,
God chose you.
Just because you're you.
How do you treat what God has chosen?

Let's look at Matthew 19:

'Go away.'
That's what Jesus' disciples say to people.
People who were bringing their children to Jesus.
In those days, children were seen as insignificant.
They had no power.
They were not even seen as fully people.
And that's probably why the disciples speak as they do.
Go away.
Don't bother Jesus with insignificant things.

But the children are not insignificant to Jesus.
He welcomes them.
He blesses them.
He values them.

The custom of the time suggested the people were bringing insignificant things to Jesus.

But they brought them anyway.
Are you like the disciples?
Thinking Jesus won't want to be bothered with things in your life that you deem insignificant?
Or are you like the people who brought their children?
Daring to believe that whatever anyone else says, Jesus will be interested.
He will be interested in your everyday hopes, worries, dreams, fears, plans.

Luke 12:7:
'The very hairs of your head are all numbered.'

You have a God who is interested.
In you.
Every bit of you.
Including the bits you don't like.
Or the bits you think are insignificant.

Isaiah 55:8 (NLT):
' "My thoughts are nothing like your thoughts," says the Lord. "And my ways are far beyond anything you could imagine." '

Eliab thought that looking after sheep was only worth mentioning with disdain.

God disagreed.

'God chose things the world considers foolish in order to shame those who think they are wise. And he chose things that are powerless to shame those who are powerful. God chose things despised by the world, things counted as nothing at all, and used them to bring to nothing what the world considers important' (1 Corinthians 1:27,28 NLT).

What else has God chosen?

'Love, joy, peace, forbearance [patience], kindness, goodness, faithfulness, gentleness and self-control' (Galatians 5).

These things are on God's heart for you.

Have you chosen them?

I have found [insert your own name], a person after my own heart, who will do everything I want them to do.

Day 17

Father God,

Thank you that your ways are not my ways.
Help me to believe that you chose me.
That you are interested in me.
Help me to keep your perspective.
In everything.
To choose what you want me to choose.
To do what you want me to do.
To always keep my heart turned towards you.

Amen

David's Aim

Turn my heart
to God

My response:

Day 18

I don't believe Eliab! I mean, can't I even speak, now? I turned away from him and spoke to someone else. They were happy to listen to me and answer my question about what Saul will do for the one who defeats Goliath. They said the same as the others had said. But I just keep getting more and more angry the more I think about it. Who does Goliath think he is? How dare he despise and ridicule and disregard God's own army?

God's army, God's very own people, were being ridiculed.
Which meant God was, too.

Come here, someone. Come and fight me!
Goliath shouted.
And the people ran.
Come on, Moses. Come here.
God called him.
And Moses went.

What's your view of God?
Someone who calls you?

Or someone who shouts at you?
Someone you go to?
Or someone who makes you run away?

Jeremiah 31:3:
'I have loved you with an everlasting love; I have drawn you with unfailing kindness.'

Let's look at Exodus:

'Bye,' chorus a crowd of people.
'Bye,' replies Moses, as he leaves them behind and sets off up a mountain.
The people know why he's going.
He's answering the call of his God.
Of their God.
The God who freed them from slavery in Egypt.
Who made a path through the sea to help them escape.
Who led them through the desert.
Who provided water to drink and food to eat.
Who gave them victory in battle.
Who 'carried them on eagles' wings and brought them to himself' (see Exodus 19:4).

Moses disappears from view.
Perhaps the people think about their God.
Time passes.
The people think about their God less frequently now.

Less and less.
Day after day, Moses is up on that mountain.
They can't see him.
And, in the end, the people give up.

They give up on God, too.
'When the people saw how long it was taking Moses
to come back down the mountain, they gathered
around Aaron. "Come on," they said, "make us some
gods who can lead us. We don't know what happened
to this fellow Moses, who brought us here from the
land of Egypt"' (Exodus 32:1 NLT).
They all got together and made a calf from melted
gold.
Then they bowed down and worshipped it.
Afterwards, they danced around it.
And that's the first thing Moses saw when he came
down from the mountain.
Fresh from meeting with the living God, he's
confronted with the living God being replaced.
Despised.
Ridiculed.

David was faced with God and his army being
despised and ridiculed.
David was angry.
Moses was angry.

How do you feel when you see God being replaced or despised or ridiculed?
By other people?
By yourself?
Does it make you angry on God's behalf?
It made Jesus angry.
Angry enough to cause mayhem in the temple (Matthew 21).
To clear out all the wrong-doing, so that God's temple was kept holy.

1 Corinthians 6:19 (NLT):
'Don't you realize that your body is the temple of the Holy Spirit, who lives in you and was given to you by God?'

Keep the temple holy.

On the mountain, God had given Moses stone tablets with writing on.
Writing which told people how to live God's way.
And now Moses was so angry that he smashed them to pieces.
Right at the foot of the mountain where he'd just met with God.

Later, God said again to Moses:
'Come here.'
So Moses climbed the mountain.

Carrying a new set of stone tablets.
And God wrote on them once more.
Different stone.
Same words.
The words hadn't changed.
God hadn't changed.
He never does.

If we don't want to ridicule God, we won't reject his guidelines on how to live.

Micah 6:8:
'And what does the LORD require of you? To act justly and to love mercy and to walk humbly with your God.'

Don't be someone who despises God.

1 Peter 1:15:
'Just as he who called you is holy, so be holy in all you do'.

And don't be someone who despises God's people.
Like Goliath.
And Eliab.
By not letting David speak, Eliab was not valuing David.
He was not acknowledging him.
Basically, Eliab was not recognizing that anyone, even his little brother David, could be a warrior for God.

Ephesians 6 talks about putting on the full armour
of God.
The helmet of salvation, the belt of truth, the
breastplate of righteousness, the shield of faith, the
shoes of peace, the sword of the Spirit.
And we need to make sure we don't forget to put
it on.
And we need to remember that others are wearing
the same armour.
Not only that, we need to remember they have as
much right to do so as anyone else.
Maybe they are different from us.
Or have different ways of doing things.
But we're in the same army.
God's army.
And, together, wearing his armour, we can live the
reality of Ephesians 6:10:
'be strong in the Lord and in his mighty power.'

Day 18

Father God,

Help me not to despise you.
Or others.
I want to honour you by living in a way that
pleases you.
In love and mercy and holiness.
I'm proud to wear your armour.
Help me to value your army as much as I do your
armour.

Amen

David's Aim

Be holy

My response:

Day 19

Well, the grapevine must have been hard at work. It seems that someone who overheard someone who overheard someone talking about the questions I've been asking has told King Saul. And Saul has sent for me. I'm off to see him now.

Acts 13:22: 'I have found David son of Jesse, a man after my own heart ...'
David's questions about Goliath reflected his thoughts.
They reflected what was going on inside him.
In his heart.
In his mind.
That God came first.
And people overheard his thoughts reflected in his questions.

If someone overheard your thoughts, what would they hear?

Colossians 3:2:
'Set your minds on things above, not on earthly things.'

Let's look at John the Baptist:

John is popular.
People flock to him, wanting to be baptized.
They follow him.
They support him.
They hang on to his every word.
And then Jesus comes along.
Some people follow Jesus instead.
Some stick with John.

One day, both groups are baptizing people at the
same time.
Plenty of people.
Plenty of water.
No problem.
But then John's followers notice that more and more
people are going to Jesus.
That can't be right.
So they go and tell John.
He'll feel as indignant as they do.
And what does John reply?

John 3:27:
*'A person can receive only what is given them
from heaven.'*

That's where John's thoughts were.
Heaven.

God.
As with David, John's words reflected his heart.
God came first.

Colossians 3:2:
'Set your minds on things above, not on earthly things.'

In Jesus, God came to live amongst us (Matthew 1:23).
As a man.
But still as God.
John had two choices before him.
Jesus, the heavenly perspective.
Or his disciples, the earthly perspective.
He chose the former.
'He [Jesus] must become greater; I must become less'
(John 3:30).
I can receive what is given me from heaven.
The privilege of having less of self in my life.
So that there can be more of Jesus.
And to live a life which echoes Paul's words really is a
privilege:

Colossians 3:3 (NLT):
'For you died to this life, and your real life is hidden with
Christ in God.'

But it's a one-or-the-other privilege.
John couldn't keep changing his mind.

'I know all the things you do, that you are neither hot nor cold. I wish that you were one or the other!' (Revelation 3:15 NLT).
It's also a privilege which leads to life.
'If you try to hang on to your life, you will lose it. But if you give up your life for my sake, you will save it' (Luke 9:24 NLT).

Which do you choose?
Heaven or earth?
Jesus or self?

God showed the perspective he chooses.
Remember what he said to Samuel, back when Samuel was choosing the king:
'People look at the outward appearance, but the LORD looks at the heart' (1 Samuel 16:7).
He chooses hearts.
Hearts that are turned towards him.

Proverbs 4:23 (NLT):
'Guard your heart above all else, for it determines the course of your life.'

The things in David's heart and mind were reported to Saul.
And they grabbed Saul's attention.
They made Saul say, 'I want to see him and talk about this further.'

Day 19

Did you know that things on your heart and mind
grab God's attention?
He wants to share them.
Whatever they are.
The bad as well as the good.
I want to see you and let's talk about this.
I'm interested.
Will you tell me more?

Proverbs 23:26:
'Give me your heart . . .'

Father God,

Thank you for what you give me from heaven.
Your perspective.
The privilege of a life hidden with you.
Sometimes I lose perspective a bit.
My self becomes more important than your self.
Help me to give you my heart.
Again and again.
And keep it hidden in yours.

Amen

David's Aim

What is my
perspective?

My response:

Day 20

This is how my conversation with Saul went:

Me: I'll go and fight Goliath.

Saul: No, you won't. You can't. You're only a boy. You have no experience and he's been fighting for years.

Me: I'm a shepherd. I've been fighting lions and bears for years. God helped me beat them and he will help me beat Goliath, this giant who is mocking God's army. I'm confident that God will rescue me.

Saul: OK, go. And God be with you.

Saul, understandably, was reluctant to be responsible for sending a boy to fight a giant.
What changed his mind?
Basically, David reminded Saul of something.
He reminded him that God is God.
And that because he's God, he helps.
Jehovah Ezer, one of God's names (Psalm 33:20), means 'The Lord our help'.

It can be easy to become complacent about God.
He can become so familiar that we lose sight of who he really is.

God is God.
All.
The.
Time.

Psalm 46:1:
'God is our refuge and strength, an ever-present help in trouble.'

David knew that God is God and he had confidence in him.
Confidence of rescue.

Let's look at Daniel 3:

A message went out.
The king has made a gold statue.
Every time you hear music, you must bow down and worship the statue.
The statue was tall, over 27 metres high.
It would have been hard to miss.
The message could have said:
Every time you see the statue, bow down and worship it.
And there would probably have been a lot of bowing down,
especially from people who saw it every day.
But, gradually, maybe the worship would have dimmed.
People would forget to bow down when they saw the statue.

Because they no longer noticed it.
It was just always there.
They'd notice if it wasn't, but they'd have stopped
noticing that it was.

What about you?
With God?
Would you notice if he wasn't there but, maybe, have
stopped noticing that he is?
God is 'ever-present'.
And not only when things are difficult.

The king made sure people wouldn't forget to notice
the statue.
His way of doing that was to play music as a reminder.
It's good to have reminders that God is God.
What's your way of doing that?
Maybe Bible notes, pictures, study groups,
bookmarks, friends, magnets on the fridge . . .

The message that went out also said that anyone who
did not bow down and worship the statue would be
thrown into a blazing furnace.
Which is why three men, Shadrach, Meshach and
Abednego, are standing before the king.
They've been summoned.
Because the king is furious with them.
'Is it true that you refuse to worship the statue?'
Yes.

'Right. You have one more chance. When you hear the music, bow down and worship the statue.
If you don't, that's it.
I'll have you thrown into the fire.
Straight away.
No god will be able to rescue you then, will they?'
Well, ours will.

Like David, the three men were confident that God would rescue them.

Daniel 3:17:
'The God we serve is able . . .'

Is your God able?
Yes.
'Now all glory to God, who is able, through his mighty power at work within us, to accomplish infinitely more than we might ask or think' (Ephesians 3:20 NLT).

Then Shadrach, Meshach and Abednego go a step further:

'But even if he doesn't [rescue us], we want to make it clear to you, Your Majesty, that we will never serve your gods or worship the gold statue you have set up' (Daniel 3:18 NLT).

God is God.
Full stop.
Whether he saved them from trouble or not.
Their relationship with God did not depend on God making life easy.
It relied upon the fact that they knew he was there with them.
All the time.
Ever-present.
Ever-able.
Even in the fire.

The king did throw them into the flames.
All three of them.
And then, as the king looked, he saw four.
Four figures.
Walking around in the fire.
The fire was raging and yet they were strolling around in there.
Together.

Isaiah 43:2b (NLT):

'When you walk through the fire of oppression, you will not be burned up; the flames will not consume you.'

God, our helper, rescues us in all situations.
By being with us in them.

Rescue means to save from.
God saves us from facing things alone.

127

Confronting giants?
He's right there with you.
Oppressed by raging fire?
He's right there with you.
You're not alone.
You never are.

'God is God' is with you.

Every step.

Psalm 46:1:
'God is our refuge and strength, an ever-present help in trouble.'

Father God,

I do become complacent with you.
Help me to notice you more.
To appreciate you more.
To worship you more.
Thank you that you are with me.
Ever-able.
Ever-present.
Whatever my present holds.

Amen

David's Aim

God is God

My response:

Day 21

Before I went to fight Goliath, Saul offered me his armour. In fact, he put it on me. His tunic, armour, helmet and sword. But I couldn't even walk in them, I just kept falling over. I'm not used to them and so I told Saul I couldn't wear his things.

David, the king-in-waiting, is offered the royal armour to wear.
And it doesn't work.
It doesn't fit.
David is not king yet.
One day he will be.
But not yet.
It's not time.

It's easy to get impatient in life, isn't it?
To think we know best.
To want things now.
But sometimes God says wait.
For his timing.

Day 21

Psalm 31:15:
'My times are in your hands.'

Let's look at John 11:

Mary and Martha have a difficult situation.
Their brother is ill.
So they send for Jesus.
He'll come and sort this.
He'll make Lazarus better.
A few days later, Jesus eventually arrives.
By which time, Lazarus is in the grave.
He'd been there four days.
He didn't get better.
He died.
And Mary and Martha know why.
It's because Jesus didn't come straight away.
And maybe they are right.
But they don't know why he didn't come in their
timing.

Isaiah 55:8:
' "For my thoughts are not your thoughts, neither are
your ways my ways," declares the Lord.'

Jesus didn't come in their timing.
He came
in
God's
timing.

John tells us that Jesus loved Mary and Martha and
Lazarus.
He loved them.
But he stayed where he was for two more days before
going to them.
He could have set out two days earlier.
But he stayed.

Because he wanted to give God glory.

To show that God could raise people from the dead.
Which is what happened.
Lazarus was raised to life.
And God got the glory.

Sometimes, that's why we need to wait.
God sees the bigger picture.
We don't.
But when God doesn't do things as we'd like, it
never
ever
ever
means he doesn't love us.

Jesus loved this little family.
But he still made them wait.

David was anointed king.
But he still needed to wait until it was time for him to
be king.

Day 21

Time to wear the king's armour.
His own, not someone else's.
He tried someone else's.
And it didn't work.

1 Corinthians 12:18:
*'God has placed the parts in the body, every one of them,
just as he wanted them to be.'*

Do you sometimes wish he'd placed you differently?
Maybe even try to be placed differently?
Placed where someone else is?
But it doesn't work?
Well, there's a reason it doesn't work:
what you are in the body of Christ,
who you are in the body of Christ,
where you are in the body of Christ,
helps make the body of Christ just as God wants it
to be.
And what could be better than that?

Without you,
just as you are,
there'd be something missing.

1 Corinthians 12:4–7 (NLT):
*'There are different kinds of spiritual gifts, but the same
Spirit is the source of them all. There are different kinds
of service, but we serve the same Lord. God works in*

different ways, but it is the same God who does the work in all of us. A spiritual gift is given to each of us so we can help each other.'

God gives gifts.
For David, God had given him the gift of knowing he'd one day be king.
But he had to wait.
Martha had to wait, too.
And she received a wonderful gift in her waiting.

It was Martha to whom Jesus said,

John 11:25:
'I am the resurrection and the life.'

I am the resurrection and the life.
I overcame death.
For you.
I overcame darkness.
For you.
So live.

John 3:16:
'For God so loved the world that he gave his one and only Son, that whoever believes in him shall not perish but have eternal life.'

Day 21

Father God,

Help me to wait.
Wait for your timing.
Wait for your gifts.
Wait for your life.
To be the me you made me to be.
To know you more.
To love you more.
To live.

Amen

David's Aim

Wait with God

My response:

Day 22

I took off Saul's armour. It felt great not to be weighed down by it. Then I picked up my shepherd's bag and went to the stream. I chose five smooth stones and put them in my bag. Then I picked up my staff and sling and went out to face Goliath.

The armour is weighing David down.
So he takes it off.

What do you do when things weigh you down?
Pressures, responsibilities, worries?
Jesus says,
Let go.
Share the load.

Matthew 11:28–29 (NLT):
'Come to me, all of you who are weary and carry heavy burdens, and I will give you rest. Take my yoke upon you.'

David sets off.
Crucially, he does not turn around and try the armour again.
Does not go back and get the thing that weighed him down.

He's left it behind.
When you've shared your burdens with Jesus,
there's no need to go back to carrying them all by
yourself.

Matthew 11:29–30 (NLT):

*'Let me teach you, because I am humble and gentle at
heart, and you will find rest for your souls. For my yoke is
easy to bear, and the burden I give you is light.'*

David gets to a stream, picks up five stones and puts
them in his shepherd's bag.
Rewind a bit.
David had left his sheep in the care of someone else.
He wasn't working as a shepherd right then.
But he still carried his shepherd's bag.

Let's look at Luke 2:

Mary and Joseph are panicking.
They're sure Jesus was with them.
They saw him just a moment ago.
Didn't they?
They weave in and out of the crowd, desperately
looking for Jesus.
He's only twelve.
Too young to be lost in a crowd like this.
Mary is frantic.
Where's Jesus?

Eventually, Mary and Joseph retrace their steps.
Thinking back to the last time they saw Jesus, they
realize it was back in Jerusalem.
They hadn't seen him a moment ago, after all.
In fact, they hadn't seen him for a whole day.
They go all the way back.
And they find Jesus.
Right where they left him.

He hadn't gone anywhere.
They had.

They'd assumed Jesus was with them.
It didn't occur to them that he wasn't.
And so they didn't look.
As taking his shepherd's bag was automatic for David,
Jesus being with them was automatic for Mary and
Joseph.
So automatic that they no longer checked he was
there.
They simply assumed he was.

Which meant they didn't notice when he wasn't.

Although taking his bag was automatic for David, he
didn't forget it was there.
He actively took it with him.
He picked it up.

He noticed it was there.
The difference between assuming and taking.

Do you assume God is there,
somewhere,
in the background,
hovering around?
Or do you actively take him with you,
noticing he's there?

Psalm 16:8:

'I keep my eyes always on the LORD.'

David himself wrote these words.
Can you echo them?
I keep my eyes always on the Lord.
And David didn't only actively carry the bag with him.
He used it.
He put the stones inside, stones that would prove
vital.
Stones that were important.
Stones that needed to be kept safe.

You need to be kept safe, too.
Other people would not have seen the stones in
the bag.
But David knew they were there.

Maybe other people don't always know your life is hidden safely in God (Colossians 3:3).
But you know.
'He will cover you with his feathers, and under his wings you will find refuge' (Psalm 91:4).

David chose his stones from a stream.
Later, in Psalm 23 (NLT), he wrote: 'The LORD is my shepherd . . . he leads me beside peaceful streams.'
Peaceful here means 'resting place' (*Strong's Concordance*).
To David, streams were a place of rest.
Maybe this is even where he learned to find rest,
to seek rest,
beside streams.

Before David went out to face his giant, he spent time resting.
Preparing.
Stilling himself.
Finding peace.

Spend time coming to me, said Jesus,
and you will find rest for your souls.

Father God,

Help me to notice you're there.
Every minute.
Of every day.
You never leave me.
Help me to actively take you with me into every
situation.
And help me to remember that you offer rest.
By sharing my burdens.
Especially when they weigh me down.
Thank you that I don't have to carry them all by
myself.

Amen

David's Aim

Rest in God

My response:

Day 23

Goliath just kept coming closer to me. I thought he was big when I saw him from a distance but, up close, he is massive. He was mocking me, saying I'm only a boy and I'm treating him like a dog by coming at him with my stick. He was wearing all his armour, and his armour-bearer came too, carrying his shield and weapons for him. Well, Goliath may have all that but I have God. God is my shield. So I picked up my sling, put a stone in it, swung it round and released it. The stone flew through the air and hit Goliath right in the forehead. Then, as if in slow motion, he tumbled to the ground and lay there face down. Well and truly dead! I went and cut off his head with his own sword.

Until now, David has only seen Goliath from a distance.
And Goliath was big then.
But, up close, he's bigger than big.
Goliath is huge.

Let's look at (a different) Saul, Acts 9:

Saul knows that God is big.
But he hasn't yet seen that Jesus is God.
He sees Jesus as a threat.
Someone who people are following instead of
sticking with the old way of the law (Romans 10:4).
And he finds that hard.
Scary.
A threat.
Wrong.

Our God is big.
He's everywhere.

Psalm 139:8:

*'If I go up to the heavens, you are there; if I make my bed
in the depths, you are there.'*

How do you feel about that?
Comforted?
Or threatened?

Jesus being big goes against everything Saul has ever
known.
And so he resists it.
Saul makes it his mission to seek out and imprison
anyone who follows Jesus.
One day, he's on his way to Damascus, to throw more
Jesus-followers into jail.

As Saul travels along the road, suddenly a bright light shines all around him.
A light all the way from heaven.

In Luke 2, announcing the birth of Jesus, the glory of the Lord suddenly shone around the shepherds.
They were terrified.
And an angel gave them an instruction:
Don't be afraid.
I have good news for you:
God – in Jesus – is coming close.

God being closer than close,
being big in your life,
being present,
is good news.
You don't need to be afraid.

If you let him in, you'll see how big your God really is.
Just as it wasn't until David came close to Goliath that he saw how big he really was.

John 8:12 (NLT):

'Jesus . . . said, "I am the light of the world. If you follow me, you won't have to walk in darkness, because you will have the light that leads to life."'

So, heaven's light shines around Saul.
And suddenly, God isn't 'big in the distance' big.

Big in an 'I know he's there but he's not getting
close' big.
Big in an 'I'll resist him all the way' big.
God is right-there close.
Bigger than ever.
Saul can't resist him.
He doesn't even want to.
Because God is God is there.

Saul falls to the ground.
And then he hears a voice.
It's Jesus:
'Saul, why are you persecuting me?' (Acts 9:4 NLT).
Me.
In persecuting Jesus' followers, Saul was persecuting
Jesus himself.
Jesus felt the pain of the persecuted.
Saul's attitude to others reflected his attitude towards
Jesus.

Matthew 25:40:
*'Truly I tell you, whatever you did for one of the least of
these brothers and sisters of mine, you did for me.'*

How is your attitude towards Jesus reflected in how
you treat others?
'Saul, why are you persecuting me?'
Why are you oppressing me?
Why are you shutting me out?

Why are you keeping me at a distance?
Why?

Psalm 56:3 (NLT):
'But when I am afraid, I will put my trust in you.'

You don't need to be afraid.
If you let him in, you'll see how big your God really is.

So, there's David with his sling.
Facing a giant in full armour.
David looks Goliath up and down.
The armour gleams in the sunlight.
Sword.
Spear.
Javelin.
And David tells Goliath:
You have all that.
But I have God.

As you go through life, whatever happens, whatever comes your way, whatever you are facing, however you are feeling, remind yourself:
But I have God.
Things are hard, it's not fair etc. . . .
But I still have God.
Life feels like a battle.
But God is still with me.

Just as David wasn't alone, neither are you.

148

Day 23

1 Samuel 17:47:
'The battle is the LORD's'.

God feels the pain of the persecuted.
And he fights your battles.

Exodus 14:14:
'The LORD will fight for you; you need only to be still.'

Father God,

Thank you that you are good news.
Why do I resist good news so often?
Help me to let you stay closer than close.
Thank you that anything I go through, you do too.
My pain is your pain.
Such love overwhelms me.
Thank you that you fight for me.
I don't need to be afraid.
Thank you that you think I'm worth it.

Amen

David's Aim

Get close to God

My response:

Day 24

After I'd chopped Goliath's head off, the Philistine army turned and ran. Their hero, their champion, was dead. It was their turn to be terrified! They ran away as fast as they could, with the whole Israelite army chasing after them. Apparently, when Saul had watched me going out to fight Goliath, he'd asked the army commander whose son I was. The commander didn't know so, as soon as I returned, the commander took me to Saul. I was still holding Goliath's head. Saul asked me, 'Whose son are you?' and I told him that my dad is Jesse from Bethlehem.

Let's look at John 19:

Jesus is hanging on the cross.
He is dying.
Very soon, he'll be dead.
The pain caused by hanging on the cross would have been immense.
Excruciating.
Agonizing.
Yet Jesus looks through his pain into the crowd

around him.

And he sees someone.

Someone he's known all his life.

Mary.

His mother.

And in that instant, the thing that was uppermost in his mind was not the pain,

the humiliation,

the suffering he was enduring.

No; it was the fact that his mother would lose her son.

A relationship would be severed.

A family relationship.

A relationship which gave his mother identity.

Imagine her being asked:

'Whose mother are you?'

'Jesus'.

'He's my son.'

But now her son was going to die.

She wouldn't have a son.

She'd lose that relationship.

And with it her identity.

Who she was.

And Jesus does not want her to lose her identity.

So he uses some of his final minutes to make sure that she doesn't.

'When Jesus saw his mother there, and the disciple whom he loved standing nearby, he said to her,

Day 24

"Woman, here is your son," and to the disciple, "Here is your mother." From that time on, this disciple took her into his home' (John 19:26,27).

She's still a mother.

Her identity is secure.

On the cross, from the cross, Jesus gave Mary identity.

On the cross,
from the cross,
through the cross,
Jesus gives you identity.

'You are a chosen people, a royal priesthood, a holy nation, God's special possession' (1 Peter 2:9).

He opened wide his arms on the cross and brought you home.

Home.

To your family.

With God as your father.

If someone asked about you:

Whose child is that?

Would people know?

Or, like the army commander in Saul's army, would they be unsure?

What if someone asked the question of you:

Whose child are you?

What would you say?

Would you say 'God's, through the life-blood Jesus shed for me on the cross'?

Ephesians 2:13 (NLT):
*'Once you were far away from God, but now you have
been brought near to him through the blood of Christ.'*

What gives you identity?
Your job? Your house? Your car?
Or your relationship with God?

1 John 3:1:
*'See what great love the Father has lavished on us, that
we should be called children of God! And that
is what we are!'*

Abba Father.
God's my dad.
That's who I am.

Jesus opened wide his arms on the cross and brought
you home.

Saul wanted to know whose son David was.
David had just been out on the battlefield, alone, and
after defeating Goliath, Saul wants to know whose
son he is?
Wouldn't it be better to make it about David himself?
David's dad was not the one who stood out there and
felled a giant with a stone.
That was David.

David, who had Jesse's blood running through his veins.
Jesse, who was a part of him.
Who had made him.

Even in victory, David's identity was not in himself.
It was in his father.
And that's who Saul wanted to know about.
David's father.

Saul wanted to know about Jesse because of David's actions.
Do your actions, your life, lead people to want to know about you?
Or do they point people to God?

The God who made you who you are?
The God who gave you your gifts and talents?

Matthew 5:16 (NLT):
'In the same way, let your good deeds shine out for all to see, so that everyone will praise your heavenly Father.'

Father God,

Thank you that I can call you father.
It really is such a privilege.
Help me not to take it for granted.
Thank you that you care enough to give me
identity.
Identity in your family.
Identity in you.
Help me not to lose sight of who you made me
to be.
Or of who I am.
And to always give you the glory.

Amen

David's Aim

My identity is
in God

My response:

Day 25

I've become friends with Jonathan, Saul's son.
Well, more than friends, really. Best friends. I've
never had a friend like him and I really like it.
We just understand each other and get on so well.
Saul has been promoting me since I beat Goliath
and I now hold a high rank in the army. Everyone
seems pleased about this and I am, too. The Lord is
blessing me; whatever mission Saul sends me on is
successful.

David became friends with the king's son.
He'd have had other friends, too, but his special
friendship was with the king's son.

Who are your friends?
Making sure we spend time with other Christians is
important.

Hebrews 10:24,25:
*'Let us consider how we may spur one another on
towards love and good deeds, not giving up meeting
together, as some are in the habit of doing, but
encouraging one another'.*

Day 25

Let's look at Genesis 3:

In the Garden of Eden there lives a snake.
There also lives a woman.
Eve.
Eve and the snake are on speaking terms.
Maybe more than speaking terms.
They know each other.
So well, it seems, that they can pick up a previous
conversation midway, and carry on as though there'd
been no pause.
Last time, they were apparently discussing trees.
Because, this time, in picking up where they left off,
the snake says;
'Are you sure?
Are you sure, Eve?
That thing you told me the other day, about not
being allowed to eat fruit from the trees;
are you sure?
It's just it seems a bit odd to me.'
'Yes,' replies Eve.
'I'm sure.
But I didn't mean I'm not allowed to eat from any tree.
God said there's just one I'm not to eat from.
Actually, I'm not even allowed to touch it.
If I do, I'll die.'
'Are you being serious?
You actually believe that?
Oh, come on, Eve.

You won't die!
That fruit will make you like God;
you'll know what is good and what is evil.'

1 Corinthians 15:33:
'Do not be misled: "Bad company corrupts good character." '

The company Eve was keeping was encouraging her to distort God's definition of 'die'.
The snake meant 'you won't physically die yet'.
Which was true.
But God meant 'you will spiritually die'.
And that was true.

The snake was suggesting that in order to truly live, Eve needed to know the answers to everything.

God was saying,
You don't need to know everything.
You don't.
It's too much for you.
I know.
And that's enough.

Job 28:28 (NLT):
'The fear of the Lord is true wisdom; to forsake evil is real understanding.'

Day 25

It's important to know what we believe.
And to know who we believe.
God?
Or the world,
things,
people who try to distort God?
Who introduce doubt:
'Did God really say . . .?'

'Do not be misled: "Bad company corrupts good
character"' (1 Corinthians 15:33).

In Genesis 11, lots of people keep lots of people
company.
In fact, everyone keeps everyone company.
They move about together, sharing ideas and
speaking the same language.
One day, as they chat, they come up with a plan:

'Let's build a tower.
A really tall one that reaches all the way up to heaven.'
But God says,
No.
You're not doing that.
I'm God.
You're not.

And what does he do to remind them that he is God?
He mixes up their language.
Whilst they may still be able to communicate with each other to a degree, for true and meaningful conversation they'd instinctively gravitate towards those who shared their language.
Instinctively mix with people they understood.
With whom they had things in common.
Just as David and Jonathan did.

Who do you mix with?
People who encourage you to need to know everything?
Encourage you to try to play God?
Or people who encourage you in not needing to know everything?
Encourage you to let God be God?

'Do not be misled: "Bad company corrupts good character"' (1 Corinthians 15:33).

1 John 4:4 (NLT):
'But you belong to God, my dear children. You have already won a victory over those people, because the Spirit who lives in you is greater than the spirit who lives in the world.'

Day 25

Father God,

Help me to choose friends wisely.
To be on the alert for people and things which
distort your truth.
Thank you that I don't need to know everything.
You know it for me.
Help me to trust in that.
And not try to take your place.

Amen

David's Aim

Guard my character

My response:

Day 26

Saul and I returned home with the army after I'd killed Goliath. The women came from towns all around to meet us. They had tambourines and were singing and dancing and celebrating because of our victory over the Philistines. They were singing, 'Saul has killed thousands, David has killed tens of thousands,' and so the party goes on, everyone is having a great time!

The celebrating women were celebrating others.
The army.
The ones who'd won the victory.

Romans 12:15:
'Rejoice with those who rejoice'.

Let's look at Luke 15 again:

There's a big party going on.
Someone is being celebrated.
In style.
Everybody there wants to see him, speak to him, shake his hand.

Is it because he's a soldier come back from war?
No.
Is he perhaps an athlete who's just won a tough race?
No.
Is he a film star?
Swum the channel?
Climbed Everest?
A Michelin-starred chef?
No.
Well, what has he done, then?

He's arrived.
He's there.
He's come back.
And that's worth celebrating.

Luke 15:7 (NLT):
'There is more joy in heaven over one lost sinner who repents and returns to God than over ninety-nine others who are righteous and haven't strayed away!'

When you turn to God,
or re-turn to God,
heaven celebrates.
Not because of things you've accomplished or achieved.
Simply because you're there.
And you are worth celebrating.
Did you know that?

Zephaniah 3:17 (NLT):
'The LORD your God . . . will take delight in you with gladness . . . He will rejoice over you with joyful songs.'

People are worth celebrating.
God made people in his own image (Genesis 1:27).
God made you in his own image.
To reflect his character.
God's character in you,
who he's made you to be,
is definitely worth celebrating.

Even if you never do a single thing.

God made people and, when he saw what he had made, he declared:
'very good' (Genesis 1:31).

Do you celebrate people?
People worth celebrating simply because God made them?
Every single person on this planet deserves to be celebrated.

What can you do to show others how much they are worth?

Romans 12:10 (NLT):
'Love each other with genuine affection, and take delight in honoring each other.'

The people who went to the party planned to be there.
They left their homes and travelled to the party
venue,
all in order to celebrate someone.
Simply for being him.

The women who celebrated the Israelites' victory put
themselves out to celebrate others.
They spent time and energy preparing their dancing
and singing.
Perhaps they had to juggle their diaries.
And leave things undone.
All in order to celebrate the returning army.
Because of their victory over Goliath and the
Philistines.
Because they'd done well.

It's good to recognize when others do well.
It's good to recognize when we do well.
It's good to recognize when you do well.
God does.

Matthew 25:21:
*'His master replied, "Well done, good and faithful
servant! . . . Come and share your master's happiness!" '*

Recognize God's 'well done'.
Accept his 'well done'.
Share in the happiness it brings him.
Celebrate together.

Day 26

God.
And those he made in his image.
You.

Psalm 139:14:
*'I praise you because I am fearfully and wonderfully
made; your works are wonderful, I know that full well.'*

Father God,

Celebrating is good.
I don't celebrate enough.
Others.
Or myself.
Help me to celebrate us.
When we do things.
Or when we simply are.
Your people.
Made in your image.

Amen

David's Aim

Accept God's 'well done'

My response:

Day 27

Well, maybe not everyone was having a great
time. Saul wasn't. When he heard the song, he
was really angry, because they'd given me more
credit than him. He was jealous. Earlier on today,
I was playing my harp for him when suddenly
a spear whizzed past my head and hit the wall
right behind me. It was Saul, trying to kill me! He
threw the spear twice, but he missed both times. It
turns out that Saul is actually afraid of me. He's
sending me on more and more dangerous army
campaigns, but I have success every time because
God is helping me. The fact that God is with me
scares Saul.

Saul was jealous of David.
David was getting more recognition.

Let's look at a parable Jesus told in Matthew 20:

A man owns some land.
And he needs people to work in his vineyard.
So, early one morning, he goes to see if anyone is
looking for a job.

He spots some men and goes over to speak with them.
They agree a fee for the day – a denarius – and the labourers set to work.
A few hours later, the man goes out again.
And he sees more people waiting for work.
'You can work in my vineyard, if you like?
I'll pay you a fair wage.'
So these people set to work in the vineyard, too.
A few hours later, the same thing happens.
And again.
And again.

At the end of the day, the workers go to the landowner to collect their wages.
The ones who put in the least time are paid first.
They each receive a denarius.
'That's great,' think the ones who have worked all day.
'If they got a denarius, we'll get much more.
We've worked harder than they have.'
Reaching the front of the queue, they hold out their hands.
Expectantly.
The landowner hands over their wages.
They look down.
Disbelief.
They've got a denarius as well.
The same amount as the people who'd only turned up at the end.

'That's not fair.'

The men begin to grumble to the landowner.

'What are you doing? We worked harder than them and yet you've treated us the same?'

'He answered one of them, "Friend, I haven't been unfair! Didn't you agree to work all day for the usual wage? Take your money and go. I wanted to pay this last worker the same as you. Is it against the law for me to do what I want with my money? Should you be jealous because I am kind to others?"' (Matthew 20:13–15 NLT).

These people had a denarius.

They had what they'd been promised.

But they missed out on enjoying the promise.

Because they were so busy comparing.

In John 21, Jesus is walking along a beach with Peter.

'Peter,' he said, 'I'm giving you a special job to do for me.'

What a wonderful privilege for Peter.

Given by Jesus.

Only to Peter.

And how did he respond?

By looking away from the privilege.

His eyes fell on someone else:

But what about him?

What did Peter do?

He started comparing.

And as he did so,
as he looked away from the privilege he'd been given,
he lost some of the joy.

What about him?

Perhaps Peter was jealous.
And that made joy difficult.
Jealousy and joy don't mix.
They can't coexist.
'Anger is cruel, and wrath is like a flood, but jealousy
is even more dangerous' (Proverbs 27:4 NLT).

The workers lost out on joy that was theirs.
Peter lost out on joy that was his.
Saul lost out on joy that was his.
Because they forgot their own privilege.
And they compared.
Needlessly.

Ironically, it's possible the dancers were not singing
that David had done more than Saul.
They were singing that Saul and David had slain
thousands.
Together.
It didn't matter who had more victories than the
other.
They were a team.
Together.

Ephesians 4:16 (NLT):
'He [Christ] makes the whole body fit together perfectly. As each part does its own special work, it helps the other parts grow, so that the whole body is healthy and growing and full of love.'

Jesus said to Peter, 'Look, don't worry about him. You just follow me.'
I've given you a special part to play.
And I define what is special.
You don't.
Follow me.
Stick with me.
And you'll know joy.
Just joy.

Psalm 16:11:
'You make known to me the path of life; you will fill me with joy in your presence, with eternal pleasures at your right hand.'

Father God,

There is joy in your presence.
No place for jealousy.
Just joy.
Pure joy.
Fullness of joy.

Amen

David's Aim

Joy

My response:

Day 28

I just had a really strange message from Saul. I thought he hated me but he says he's pleased with me. In fact, he wants me to marry his daughter, Princess Michal, and become his son-in-law. I know I should be honoured but, actually, I'm confused. I mean, I can't marry the king's daughter. Apparently, she says she is in love with me, but I'm only an ordinary man. Yes, I know I'll be king one day, but not yet. How can I marry a princess?

David receives a message.
From the king.
Saul sends messengers to David:
I'm pleased with you, David.
The messengers expect David to be excited by their news.
By the honour bestowed on him.
But David isn't.
He is humbled.
He responds to the messengers:
'Do you think this is a small thing?' (See 1 Samuel 18:23.)

To be honoured by the king.
To be told the king is pleased with me?
That I give the king pleasure.
Is that a small thing?
Something I can take for granted?
Or is it a big deal?
Something I should be in awe of?

Isaiah 43:4:

'You are precious and honoured in my sight, and . . .
I love you.'

You are precious and honoured and loved by God.
By Jesus.
The King of kings.
Is that a small thing?
Or is it a big deal?
'When I consider your heavens, the work of your
fingers, the moon and the stars, which you have set in
place, what is mankind that you are mindful of them,
human beings that you care for them?' (Psalm 8:3,4).

It's a big deal.
You are precious and honoured and loved by God.

What gives God pleasure?
Well, let's start with what doesn't give him pleasure.
'He takes no pleasure . . . in human might' (Psalm
147:10 NLT).

Human strength.
God does not take pleasure in us doing things in our
own strength.
When he sees you facing life without him,
your daily ups and downs,
it does not give him pleasure.
Why?
Because he doesn't like to see you struggle.

The God who said,
Whatever you go through, I'm here (see Isaiah 43:2–13)
does not take pleasure in being told, through word or
action:
Well, I don't want you to be.

What message do your words and actions send to
God?
He takes no pleasure . . . in human might.

Why else doesn't God take pleasure in us doing things
in our own strength?
Psalm 147 tells us:
He created everything.
Including you.
He sustains everything.
Including you.
He knows and understands everything.
Including you.
There's nothing God cannot do.

'The God who made the world and everything in it is the Lord of heaven and earth and does not live in temples built by human hands. And he is not served by human hands, as if he needed anything. Rather, he himself gives everyone life and breath and everything else' (Acts 17:24,25).
He doesn't need us to 'do' anything.

Psalm 147:10 (NLT):
'He takes no pleasure . . . in human might.'

'No, the LORD's delight is in those who fear him, those who put their hope in his unfailing love' (verse 11).
Bring him delight by fearing him.
The Hebrew word translated 'fear' here means 'worship'.
When you worship God, your worship brings him pleasure.
Brings him joy.

Did you know that?

The first of God's Ten Commandments says:
'You shall have no other gods before me'
(Exodus 20:3).

Including making a 'god before me' of your own strength.
Your own abilities.
Your own ideas.

Put God first.
Bring him joy.
Have no other gods before him.
Nothing more important to you than God.
That's worship.

Bring him delight by hoping in his love.
Even when it's tough.

Jeremiah 31:3 (NLT):
'I have loved you, my people, with an everlasting love.
With unfailing love I have drawn you to myself.'

That's what you can hope in.
The fact that you're precious and honoured and loved
with a love that
never,
ever
fails.

Father God,

Thank you that you honour me.
Help me to appreciate what that really means.
You. Honour. Me.
I want to honour you, too.
So often I try to do things in my own strength.
I know that doesn't honour you.
But I do it anyway.
I'm sorry, Father.
Help me to bring you pleasure
by living to worship you.

Amen

David's Aim

Live in worship

My response:

Day 29

Oh right. It seems that there is a price I'll have to pay to marry Michal. Saul wants 100 Philistine foreskins! I'm sure he's planning that I'll die in my attempt to kill these Philistines. Well, you know what; I'll show him! I'm going to do even more. I'm going to get 200. Why shouldn't I become the king's son-in-law?

Here is a classic example of going above and beyond.
Saul wants 100.
So David says, I'll give him 200.
Saul thought 100 was a big ask.
Almost an impossible ask.
But David decides to give him more.
In a sense, by only asking for 100, Saul had put a limitation on what he thought David could do.

Let's look at Malachi 3:

God is recounting a conversation to the Israelites.
The conversation involves God himself and the people of Israel.
God's chosen people (Psalm 135:4).

God begins by saying: 'You people are robbing me.'
You're stealing from me.
And the people don't know what he means.
What's God talking about?
They demand to know just how he thinks they are
robbing him.

The people were not tithing.

God had commanded them to tithe;
to give God a tenth of all they had.
Crops, money, things . . .
And, over the years, the tenth had dwindled.
It had become less than a tenth.
It seems the people had stopped trusting God.
If they gave a whole tenth away, what would they
have to fall back on if they hit hard times?
Better to keep some for themselves, just in case.

And God says,
No.
Look.
Come on, you can trust me.
Tell you what, put it to the test.
Give me the whole tithe and you'll see.

Malachi 3:10 (NLT):
*'I will open the windows of heaven for you. I will pour out
a blessing so great you won't have enough room to take
it in! Try it! Put me to the test!'*

186

Saul limited what he thought David could do.
The Israelites limited what they thought God could do.

Do you limit God?
Allow him to be God but only within the confines of
your own expectations?
Your own perception of what he can do rather than
what he can actually do?
What he can actually be trusted with?

Which is everything.
The whole tithe.
Not just part of it.

Imagine knowing so much blessing that you can't
even begin to grasp it all.
Stop limiting God and you won't need to imagine.
Because you'll know.

I will open the windows of heaven for you.
I will pour out a blessing so great you won't have enough
room to take it in!
Try it!
Put me to the test!

David exceeded Saul's expectations.
Because Saul did not know David well enough to
know what David could do.

God knows you well enough to know exactly what you can do.

We know that he doesn't need you to do anything.
But that doesn't mean he wouldn't like you to.
In his strength.
He won't ask you to do things you can't do.
In his strength.

Philippians 4:13:
'I can do all this through him who gives me strength.'

What God does ask you to do may test you.
As the Israelites were tested.

Were they willing to release it all to God, rather than hold some back?

Are you willing?
Feelings,
money,
time,
things?

The Israelites would not see blessing until they released the tithe to God.
Things they kept for themselves.
But, if they let those things go, then they'd see blessing.

More than see it.
It would surround them.
In every way.

Do you need to let go?
Of things, people, feelings, attitudes . . .?
If God says let go,
let go.
So he can bless you more.

David moves from not believing it's valid for him to
become the king's son-in-law
to believing that it is.
And then David is 'pleased to become the king's
son-in-law' (1 Samuel 18:26).

He didn't have to do what the king asked.
He didn't have to become part of the royal family.
He didn't have to be pleased to become the king's
son-in-law.
But he was.

You don't have to trust God.

You don't have to become part of God's family.
You don't have to be pleased that God wants you to
be his child.
But will you be?
Are you?
God wants you to be.

Acts 17:26–28 (NLT):

*'From one man he created all the nations throughout
the whole earth. He decided beforehand when they
should rise and fall, and he determined their boundaries.
His purpose was for the nations to seek after God
and perhaps feel their way toward him and find
him – though he is not far from any one of us. For in him
we live and move and exist. As some of your own poets
have said, "We are his offspring."'*

God is not far from any one of us.

He's not far from you.

Ever.

Day 29

Father God,

I know you are rich.
And I know you are generous.
More than generous.
You want to bless me so much.
Yet I still limit you.
I hold things back, just in case.
Help me to give you all you ask.
To make all of me available.
To let go.
In your strength.
And receive blessing.

Amen

David's Aim

Open my hands

My response:

Day 30

I'm married now! Michal loves me and Jonathan is still my best friend. God is really with me, making me successful in every battle I fight. My life is so different from what it used to be, but it is still good. The only downside is that Saul is still afraid of me. I don't think that will ever change.

Imagine the news headlines:
Hills to palace.
Shepherd boy marries princess.

The shepherd boy was called David.
David means 'beloved'.
The prince was called David.
David means 'beloved'.

David's circumstances changed.
Dramatically.
But his name didn't.
It wasn't shortened to Dave when he was a shepherd and double-barrelled to David-David when he was a prince.
No.

He was David.
Beloved.
Whatever was happening in his life.

When he was looking after his sheep,
David was beloved.
When he was not invited to the celebration at home,
David was beloved.
When he was snubbed by his brother,
David was beloved.
When he was ridiculed by Goliath,
David was beloved.
When he defeated the giant,
David was beloved.
When he found a good friend in Jonathan,
David was beloved.
When Saul tried to kill him,
David was beloved.
David was beloved at all times.

And so are you.

Lamentations 3:22,23 (NLT):

'The faithful love of the LORD never ends! His mercies never cease. Great is his faithfulness; his mercies begin afresh each morning.'

Each morning.
Whatever each day holds,
it is full of love.
From God to you.
So be loved.

Saul could see that God was with David.
Why?
Because David was different.
David lived his name.
Beloved.
All the time.
He was beloved by God.
Do you really know that you are, too?
David knew he was beloved by God.
Did you really know that you can know it, too?
Because you are.

1 Thessalonians 1:4 (NLT):
*'We know, dear brothers and sisters, that God loves you
and has chosen you to be his own people.'*

When others see you, do they see that you belong to
God?
That he is with you?
That you're beloved?

David was beloved by God.
And it showed.
In his reliance on God.
In his humility.
In his obedience.
In his refusal to let God be defied.

As he entered royal life, with all that lay ahead, David
needed to know he was beloved.
To know he was not alone.
To know that God was with him.

As you enter the next part of your life, whatever it
holds, you can know the same.
Be assured of that.

Deuteronomy 31:8:

*'The L*ORD* himself goes before you and will be with you;
he will never leave you nor forsake you. Do not be afraid;
do not be discouraged.'*

And don't forget;
like David,
you are
every day
beloved.

Day 30

Father God,

Thank you for David.
For his faith in you.
For his trust in your bigness.
His giant was tiny compared with you.
And David knew it.
Help me to know the same when my giants come.
Thank you that you call me beloved.
Help me to live in the light of your heart.
Just as David did.

Amen

David's Aim

Live beloved

My response: